Sherwood Anderson
on
Life and Writing

Selected by Anna Maria Caldara

ISBN-13: 978-1532863646
ISBN-10: 1532863640

Cover: The cover photo shows a vintage hooked rug based on one of Sherwood Anderson's watercolors entitled "A Blue Ridge Road in Virginia." It was produced by Rosemont Industries of Marion, Virginia, U.S.A., which was founded by Laura Lu Copenhaver (Sherwood Anderson's mother-in-law.) The rug was presented to Dr. Welford Taylor by her daughter, Eleanor Copenhaver Anderson. It appears here solely through the courtesy of Dr. Taylor, to whom I extend my utmost gratitude.

To the man himself

My appreciation to…

the late **Hope Anwyll,** and **Tom Nelson**, for the use of their copier early in this project; **Martha Briggs, Alison Hinderliter**, and **Dr. David Spadafora** of The Newberry Library, Chicago, Illinois, U.S.A., for their gracious assistance; **Brian Carroll**, **Bill McLaughlin**, and **Daniel Waterman** for encouragement; **Megan Conrad**, for technical expertise with a smile, and the **Conrad** family for precious time spent without her; **Tom Copenhaver**, for opening Ripshin, and letting us linger; to the estates of, and to the late **Howard Mumford Jones** and the late **Walter Rideout**, selectors and editors of the *Letters of Sherwood Anderson*, for reproduction of their footnotes; **Mike Spear** of **The Sherwood Anderson Foundation**, for august guidance; **Craig Tenney** of Harold Ober Associates, and **Harold Ober Associates**, for permission to reprint Sherwood Anderson's words;

…and especially to **Dr. Welford Taylor**, whose unbounded generosity of spirit pushed this project forward.

"...to catch and hold my own note out of the jar and jangle of noises."

--Letter to Waldo Frank, ? March, 1917, from *Letters of Sherwood Anderson*, #7

CHAPTERS

Foreword

At the age of 15, on the pages of a high school text book, I met Sherwood Anderson. "A Story Teller's Story" startled me.

I was sitting in a classroom, in a row. The classroom was square, the blackboard was rectangular. Everything was as it usually is in a building constructed for the business of learning...including the presence of boredom and anger. They were as much in the classroom as if those words had been branded onto the bricks.

It was the late 1960s in the eastern United States. Students were being drafted and shipped to Vietnam. We were too young to vote, yet old enough to die. Pollution was weakening Mother Earth. The violence of racism was igniting war in the streets. Why were people content to let injustice reign? We who protested the order of the day felt misunderstood by our parents, and society. Very little we were being taught in our Institution of Higher Learning seemed relevant, let alone *startlingly* relevant!

Outside was a hedge, a lawn, and the school driveway. Then the road, and a forest. In-between the forest and a hill was a railroad track.

That railroad track was my corridor for fantasies. I savored the muffled roar of the approaching diesel, shielded by the trees. Soon a shivering whine pierced the air of the classroom. It forced the teacher to talk louder. My ears embraced the droning forward thrust of the engines as the necklace of boxcars rattled behind them. Again the whistle floated through the walls. Scraping and screeching faded as the train trundled by.

I was dreaming of the boxcars...Jersey Central, Norfolk and Western...perhaps coupled together in the Mid-West, their orange or blue or crimson sides splattered with dirt and graffiti. I was inside a boxcar, hopping the train. From its open doors the sun illuminated passing foliage.

Before reading Sherwood Anderson, my life had been a railroad track clamped to the ground. Walt Whitman, Thoreau, Emerson, and Frederick Douglass had loosened some of the bolts. Now the rails jumped a little when the train bore down. The engineer had to move slowly, as the path was no longer smooth.

During "A Story Teller's Story," Sherwood Anderson positioned his foot on one of my rails. He grasped the switch above it with both hands and he pulled. With the might of his words, he threw the switch. The train of my life changed direction.

What was it that Sherwood Anderson had uttered? He had been married, had three children, was working in a paint factory. Outwardly he was taking care of his family and living a "good life." But secretly he yearned to be a writer. The desire clawed at him until he could not bear to suppress it. One day he left his job, and his family. He hopped trains and lived and worked with laborers. When all around him slept, he wrote. He tried desperately to convey in words the alienation of those who are different; workers' dignity robbed by Industrialization; the spiritual vacancy left by the loss of farms; and the writer struggling to excel at writing, earn an honest living by writing, and engage one's talent to further justice.

Did he succeed? Although upheld as a pillar of literature, Sherwood Anderson would probably say that he did not often succeed. He read great writers. He tortured himself to express his own voice. But the moments when he broke through were overshadowed by hours of inability to connect his thoughts with words befitting the Muse.

Still, "It is ten times more important to be devoted as it is to succeed," Sherwood Anderson said. For in that unwavering allegiance to Art lies the key. Oh, probably not the key to monetary independence. Rather, the ability to glean, from one's own words put to paper, a slice of the Truth. (Is the pursuit of Truth worth a lifetime of monumental effort, and self-doubt? If not, would we have beacons to dissipate the gloom of untruth?)

Sherwood Anderson's efforts to hone the craft of writing rather than succumb to popular sales planted the idea for this book. While reading *Sherwood Anderson's Notebook* (published 1926), *Sherwood Anderson's Memoirs* (published 1942), and *Letters of Sherwood Anderson* (published 1953), I noticed the author's acute observations about this temptation, which every writer faces. I decided to mark and categorize these passages, realizing what an insight they were into the art.

But Sherwood Anderson was not sure he could give anyone advice about writing. That is significant. So many others are cocksure.

He never sought an advanced degree in writing. Ah, the seduction of a university that presents one with a certificate at the end of a semester, a year, five or ten years! Such papers seek to convince the graduate that he or she is more of a writer than a high school drop-out with a pen and a pad of paper. The words of another writer whom publishers ignored--Walt Whitman-- inspired Sherwood Anderson: "...go freely with powerful uneducated persons...re-examine all you have been told in school or church or in any book..."

Sherwood Anderson was not the last writer to change my life. Zora Neale Hurston, Emma Goldman, Alice Paul, and Charlotte Perkins Gilman came later, as did others. But his willingness to risk everything to match his ink with Truth emboldened me. His straightforwardness about frustration, and fear of financial ruin, prepared me for my own path with the pen.

There is a point on the horizon when one is walking railroad tracks--a point where the rails seem to merge. From that point materializes the blurry glow of the headlight...the vibration underfoot...the subdued rumble...the oily fumes. When that point is reached, another one appears, and then another; and so it goes.

We will imagine that we have walked to the first point. This is where my words end, and Sherwood Anderson's begin. After that, you must find your own words.

Anna Maria Caldara

Foreword by Sherwood Anderson

It sometimes seems to me that I should prepare a book designed to be read by other and younger writers. This not because of accomplishment on my part, but because of the experiences, the particular experiences, I have had.

It is so difficult for most of us to realize how fully and completely commercialism enters into the arts. For example, how are you to know that really the opinion of the publisher or the magazine editor in regard to your work, what is a story and what isn't, means nothing? Some of my own stories, for example, that have now become almost American classics, that are put before students in our schools and colleges as examples of good storytelling, were, when first written, when submitted to editors, and when seen by some of the so-called outstanding American critics, declared not stories at all.

It is true they were not nice little packages, wrapped and labeled in the O. Henry manner. They were obviously written by one who did not know the answers. They were simple little tales of happenings, things observed and felt. There were no cowboys or daring wild game hunters. None of the people in the tales got lost in burning deserts or went seeking the North Pole. In my stories I simply stayed at home, among my own people, wherever I happened to be, people in my own street. I think I must, very early, have realized that this was my milieu, that is to say, common everyday American lives. The ordinary beliefs of the people about me, that love lasted indefinitely, that success meant happiness, simply did not seem true to me.

Things were always happening. My eyes began to see, my ears to hear. Most of our American storytelling at that time had concerned only the rich and the well-to-do. I was a storyteller but not yet a writer of stories. As I came of a poor family, older men were always repeating to me the old saying,

"Get money. Money makes the mare go."

For a time I was a laborer. As I had a passion for fast trotting and pacing horses, I worked about race tracks. I became a soldier, I got into business.

I knew, often quite intensively, Negro swipes about race tracks, small gamblers, prize fighters, common laboring men and women. There was a violent, dangerous man, said to be a killer. One night he walked and talked to me and became suddenly tender. I was forced to realize that all sorts of emotions went on in all sorts of people. A young man who seemed outwardly a very clod suddenly began to run wildly in the moonlight. Once I was walking in a wood and heard the sound of a man weeping. I stopped, looked, and listened. There was a farmer who, because of ill luck, bad weather, and perhaps even poor management, had lost his farm. He had gone to work in a factory in town, but, having a day off, had returned secretly to the fields he loved. He was on his knees by a low fence, looking across the fields in which he had worked from boyhood. He and I were employed at the time in the same factory, and in the factory he was a quiet, smiling man, seemingly satisfied with his lot.

I began to gather these impressions. There was a thing called happiness toward which men were striving. They never got to it. All of life was amazingly accidental. Love, moments of tenderness and despair, came to the poor and the miserable as to the rich and successful.

It began to seem to me that what was most wanted by all people was love, understanding. Our writers, our storytellers, in wrapping life up into neat little packages were only betraying life. It began to seem to me that what I wanted for myself most of all, rather than so-called success, acclaim, to be praised by publishers and editors, was to try to develop, to the top of my bent, my own capacity to feel, see, taste, smell, hear. I wanted, as all men must want, to be a free man, proud of my own manhood, always more and more aware of earth, people, streets, houses, towns, cities. I wanted to take all into myself, digest what I could.

I could not give the answers, and so for a long time when my stories began to appear, at first only in little highbrow magazines, I was almost universally condemned by the critics. My stories, it seemed, had no definite ends. They were not conclusive and did not give the answers, and so I was called vague. "Groping" was a favorite term. It seems I could not get a formula and stick to it. I could not be smart about life. When I wrote my Winesburg stories—for the whole series I got eighty-five dollars—such critics as Mr. Floyd Dell and Henry Mencken, having read them, declared they were not stories. They were merely, it seemed, sketches. They were too vague, too groping. Some ten or fifteen years after Mr. Mencken told me they were not stories, he wrote, telling of how, when he first saw them, he realized their strength and beauty. An imagined conversation between us, that never took place, was spoken about.

And for this I did not blame Mr. Mencken. He thought he had said what he now thinks he said.

There was a time when Mr. Dell was, in a way, my literary father. He and Mr. Waldo Frank had been the first critics to praise some of my earlier work. He was generous and warm. He, with Mr. Theodore Dreiser, was instrumental in getting my first book published. When he saw the Winesburg stories, he, however, condemned them heartily. He was at that time, I believe, deeply under the influence of Maupassant. He advised me to throw the Winesburg stories away. They had no form. They were not stories. A story, he said, must be sharply definite. There must be a beginning and an end. I remember very clearly our conversation. "If you plan to go somewhere on a train and start for the station, but loiter along the way, so that the train comes into the station, stops to discharge and take on passengers, and then goes on its way, and you miss it, don't blame the locomotive engineer," I said. I daresay it was an arrogant saying, but arrogance is also needed.

And so I had written, let us say, the Winesburg stories. The publisher who had already published two of my early novels refused them, but at last I found a publisher. The stories were called unclean, dirty, filthy, but they did grow into the American consciousness, and presently the same critic who had condemned them began asking why I did not write more Winesburg stories.

I am telling you all of this, I assure you, not out of bitterness. I have had a good life, a full, rich life. I am still having a full, rich life. I tell it only to point out to you, a young writer, filled as I am made aware by your letter to me, of tenderness for life, I tell it simply to suggest to you plainly what you are up against. For ten or fifteen years after I had written and published the Winesburg stories, I was compelled to make my living outside of the field of writing. You will find none of my stories even yet in the great popular magazines that pay high prices to writers.

I do not blame the publishers or the editors. Once I was in the editorial rooms of a great magazine. They had asked me in for an editorial conference.

Would it not be possible for them to begin publishing my stories?

I advised against it. "If I were you, I would let Sherwood Anderson alone."

I had been for a long time an employee of a big advertising agency. I wrote the kind of advertisements on which great magazines live.

But I had no illusions about advertising, could have none. I was an advertising writer too long. The men employed with me, the businessmen, many of them successful and even rich, were like the laborers, gamblers, soldiers, race track swipes I had formerly known. Their guards down, often over drinks, they told me the same stories of tangled, thwarted lives.

How could I throw a glamor over such lives? I couldn't.

The Winesburg stories, when first published, were bitterly condemned. In one New England town, where three copies of the book had been bought, they were publicly burned in the public square of the town. I remember a letter I once received from a woman. She had been seated beside me at the table of a friend. "Having sat beside you and having read your stories, I feel that I shall never be clean again," she wrote. I got many such letters.

Then a change came. The book found its way into schools and colleges. Critics who had ignored or condemned the book now praised it.

"It's Anderson's best work. It is the height of his genius. He will never again do such work."

People constantly came to me, all saying the same thing.

"But what else of mine have you read since?"

A blank look upon faces.

They had read nothing else of mine. For the most part they were simply repeating, over and over, an old phrase picked up.

Now, I do not think all of this matters. I am one of the fortunate ones. In years when I have been unable to make a living with my pen, there have always been friends ready and willing to help me. There was one man who came to me in a year when I felt, when I knew, that I had done some of my best and truest work, but when, no money coming in, I was trying to sell my house to get money to live.

He wanted, he said, one of my manuscripts. "I will lend you five thousand dollars." He did lend it, knowing I could never return his money, but he did not deceive me. He had an affection for me as I had for him. He wanted me to continue to live in freedom. I have found this sort of thing among the rich as well as the poor. My house where I live is filled with beautiful things, all given to me. I live well enough. I have no quarrel with life.

And I am only writing all this to you to prepare you. In a world controlled by business why should we not expect businessmen to think first of business?

And do bear in mind that publishers of books, of magazines, of newspapers are, first of all, businessmen. They are compelled to be.

And do not blame them when they do not buy your stories. Do not be romantic. There is no golden key that unlocks all doors. There is only the joy of living as richly as you can, always feeling more, absorbing more, and if you are by nature a teller of tales, the realization that by faking, trying to give people what they think they want, you are in danger of dulling and in the end quite destroying what may be your own road into life.

There will remain for you, to be sure, the matter of making a living, and I am sorry to say to you that in the solution of that problem, for you and other young writers, I am not interested. That, alas, is your own problem. I am interested in only what you may be able to contribute to the advancement of our mutual craft.

But why not call it an art? That is what it is.

Did you ever hear of an artist who had an easy road to travel in life?

-- Letter to George Freitag*, August 27, 1938, from *Letters of Sherwood Anderson*, #342

*George Freitag of Canton, Ohio, entered into correspondence with Anderson in the summer of 1938 on problems of the young writer. He published "The Transaction" in the *Atlantic* for August, 1938.

Chapter One

The Purpose
Why do we write?

The writer is seeking a certain tune, a rhythm. When he has caught it the words and sentences flow freely. There is a new cunning, a new majesty to his thoughts. To speak of him as working is absurd. As well speak of a stream working as it flows down to the sea.

--from *Sherwood Anderson's Notebook*, Note 19

About the *Winesburg, Ohio* stories:

...The stories belonged together. I felt that, taken together, they made something like a novel, a complete story. There was all of this starved side of American small town life. Perhaps I was even vain enough to think that these stories told would, in the end, have the effect of breaking down a little the curious separateness of so much of life, these walls we build up about us. I thought of our puritanism. It seemed to lead so inevitably to hypocrisy.

The publishing house of John Lane did not want them. Naturally I thought Lane all wrong. I considered then, as I now consider, that my earlier stories, both *Windy McPherson* and at least in the writing, *Marching Men*, had been the result not so much of my own feeling about life as of reading the novels of others. There had been too much H.G. Wells, that sort of thing. I was being too heroic. I came down off my perch. I have even sometimes thought that the novel form does not fit an American writer, that it is a form which had been brought in. What is wanted is a new looseness; and in *Winesburg* I had made my own form. There were individual tales but all about lives in some way connected. By this method I did succeed, I think, in giving the feeling of the life of a boy growing into young manhood in a town. Life is a loose flowing thing. There are no plot stories in life. I had begun writing of the little lives I knew, the people I had lived, walked and talked with, perhaps even slept with.

There is still another sense in which I believe that the little stories are as revolutionary as anything I shall ever be able to write.

You do not need to go far back into the history of writing to come to the place where the life of a common man or woman, the worker, was not thought interesting. Such lives were not thought of as material for the story teller. In the old fiction, old poetry, old plays, the workers and peasants were invariably introduced as comic figures. Go to Shakespeare and you will see what I mean. It is so in all the older fiction. The notion that the worker in the factory, in the sweatshop, in the mine, or any one of the obscure figures, in any American town, might be as sensitive and as easily hurt as the well-to-do man or woman, and that the strange thing in life we call beauty might be as alive in such a one—man or woman—as in the rich and successful, is still new.

If our present capitalist system did in fact produce, even for the few, the kind of glowing lives some of our romancers pretend, I would myself hesitate about deserting capitalism. It doesn't.

And I believe that those who call themselves revolutionists will get the most help out of such men as myself by not trying to utilize such talents as we have directly for propaganda but in leaving us as free as possible to strike with our stories of American life into a deeper soil.

I mean that the lives of those who now succeed in getting money and power in our present individualistic capitalistic society are neither happy nor successful lives. That illusion needs to be destroyed.

When it comes to the others, the workers, the real producers, the downtrodden people, theirs are the stories that need to be told.

I think I have always wanted to tell their stories and still want to tell them. It is my one great passion. If *Winesburg, Ohio* tried to tell the story of the defeated figures of an old American individualistic small town life, then my later books have been but an attempt to carry these same people forward into the new American life, into the whirl and roar of modern machines. I do not believe my own impulses have changed.

--from *Sherwood Anderson's Memoirs*, "Book IV, The Literary Life, Waiting for Ben Huebsch"

I write songs and walk in a kind of wonder of unexpressed things.

--Sherwood Anderson to Waldo Frank, ? April, 1917, from *Letters of Sherwood Anderson*, #12

I have set out on a certain road, knowing very well that what I want to do will not bring me much money. If I were to spend my energy in another direction, I might get money aplenty.

Very well. I plan to get something money will not buy. It evens up fairly well.

--Sherwood Anderson to George Sylvester Viereck*, March 21, 1925, from *Letters of Sherwood Anderson*, #112

*George Sylvester Viereck, b.1884, was then editing the *American Monthly*, formerly the *Fatherland*.

Will love of words be lost? Success, standardization, big editions, money rolling in.

When you get money you are respectable.

What has respectability to do with loving words? What words do you love? Who has passed on them? What authority has said they are respectable?

Words for every act of the body, for dark and gay thoughts.

The little singing sound made by a pen on paper. The tale whispered in the night and then forgotten.

Words going the way of the blacks, of song and dance.

Can you imagine sweet words in a factory, sing them, dance them?

In the end they will make factory hands of us writers too.

The whites will get us. They win.

Don't turn your back on the modern world. Sing that too, if you can, while the sweet words last.

--from *Sherwood Anderson's Notebook*, Note 10

For a long time I have believed that crudity is an inevitable quality in the production of a really significant present-day American literature. How indeed is one to escape the obvious fact that there is as yet no native subtlety of thought or living among us? And if we are a crude and childlike people how can our literature hope to escape the influence of that fact? Why indeed should we want it to escape?   If you are in doubt as to the crudity of thought in America, try an experiment. Come out of your offices, where you sit writing and thinking, and try living with us. Get on a train at Pittsburgh and go west to the mountains of Colorado. Stop for a time in our towns and cities. Stay for a week in some Iowa corn-shipping town and for another week in one of the Chicago clubs. As you loiter about read our newspapers and listen to our conversations, remembering, if you will, that as you see us in the towns and cities, so we are. We are not subtle enough to conceal ourselves and he who runs with open eyes through the Mississippi Valley may read the story of the Mississippi Valley.

It is a remarkable story and we have not yet begun to tell the half of it. A little, I think, I know why. It is because we who write have drawn ourselves away. We have not had faith in our own people and in the story of our people. If we are crude and childlike that is our story and our writing men must learn to dare to come among us until they know the story. The telling of the story depends, I believe, upon their learning that lesson and accepting that burden.

To my room, which is on a street near the loop in the city of Chicago, come men who write. They talk and I talk. We are fools. We talk of writers of the old world and the beauty and subtlety of the work they do. Below us the roaring city lies like a great animal on the prairies, but we do not run out to the prairies. We stay in our rooms and talk.

And so, having listened to talk and having myself talked overmuch, I grow weary of talk and walk in the streets. As I walk alone an old truth comes home to me and I know that we shall never have an American literature until we return to faith in ourselves and to the facing of our own limitations. We must, in some way, become in ourselves more like our fellows, more simple and real.

For surely it does not follow that because we Americans are a people without subtlety we are a dull or uninteresting people. Our literature is dull but we are not. Remember how Dostoievsky had faith in the simplicity of the Russians and what he achieved. He lived and he expressed the life of his time and people. The thing that he did brings hope of achievement for our men.

But we should first of all accept certain truths. Why should we Americans aspire to an appearance of subtlety that belongs not to us but to old lands and places? Why talk of intellectuality and of intellectual life when we have not accepted the life we have? There is death on that road and following it has brought death into much of American writing. Can you doubt what I say? Consider the smooth slickness of the average magazine story. There is often great subtlety of plot and phrase but there is no reality. Can such work be important? The answer is that the most popular magazine story or novel does not live in our minds for a month.

And what are we to do about it? To me it seems that as writers we shall have to throw ourselves with greater daring into life. We shall have to begin to write out of the people and not for the people. We shall have to find within ourselves a little of that courage. To continue along the road we are traveling is unthinkable. To draw ourselves apart, to live in little groups and console ourselves with the thought that we are achieving intellectuality is to get nowhere. By such a road we can hope only to go on producing a literature that has nothing to do with life as it is lived in these United States.

To be sure the doing of the thing I am talking about will not be easy. America is a land of objective writing and thinking. New paths will have to be made. The subjective impulse is almost unknown to us. Because it is close to life it works out into crude and broken forms. It leads along a road that such American masters of prose as James and Howells did not want to take but if we are to get anywhere we shall have to travel the road.

The road is rough. Who, knowing our America and understanding the life in our towns and cities, can close his eyes to the fact that life here for the most part is an ugly affair? As a people we have given ourselves to industrialism and industrialism is not lovely. If anyone can find beauty in an American factory town I wish he would show me the way. For myself I cannot find it. To me, and I am living in industrial life, the whole thing is as ugly as modern war. I have to accept that fact and I believe a great step forward will have been taken when it is more generally accepted.

--from *Sherwood Anderson's Notebook*, "An Apology for Crudity"

Dear Mrs. Harriet Martin: When your brother Mike was over here last Sunday, I told him that while I would be very glad to read your stories, I felt that the probabilities were strong that I could be of very little help to you. I rather got it from Mike that what you are after principally was to do what is called "crashing the magazine market," and I have never much had this aim, nor have I ever been to much extent a magazine writer. I rather came into writing by the back door. Writing seemed to give me more satisfaction than anything else I could do, and what reputation I have got is rather, I think, a literary rather than a popular one.

I will not try to go into a detailed discussion of your stories, because I feel I am incapable of doing so, but it does seem to me, from my point of view, that yours is wrong.

I have read with a good deal of interest the letters to you from the man Uzzell*, and it seems to me that when the characters of stories are taken from this point of view—a character in one of your stories, for example, who is a farmer, suddenly turned into a lawyer, a doctor, or something else in order to fit into some plot—there isn't much left of the character. It does not seem to me that it is right or fair to people to push them about in this way. A farmer is a farmer, a lawyer a lawyer, a doctor a doctor. It seems to me that the duty of the storyteller is to study people as they are and try to find the real drama of life just as people live and experience it. In other words, I feel that the obligation to imagined characters is exactly the same as the obligation to real characters in real life.

If I were advising a young writer who really wanted to get any satisfaction out of writing and who was willing to rather give up the idea of immediate success, I would certainly tell them to spend their time studying people and in not trying to think out plots. It seems to me that the stories and the drama of the stories should come out of the real lives of people, and that there is something false and wrong in this shoving imagined people around in this way; but, as I tried to tell Mike, any success coming to a writer out of this kind of work is likely to come slowly. You will have to get what satisfaction you get out of the work itself.

Now, I am very sorry that I cannot go at your stories as a Mr. Uzzell would do, for to tell you the truth, I do not much believe in the

*Thomas H. Uzzell (1884-), "professional adviser and instructor of American writers since 1920."

Uzzells of the writing world. I tried to tell Mike that, but am afraid I did not make myself very clear, and perhaps I am not making myself clear to you.

If I were a young writer, also it seems to me I would study, not the work of the tricky, flashy magazine writers, but of the masters of the craft. I would read the stories of Chekhov, such books as (Turgenev's) *Annals of a Sportsman*, and books of that kind. If you are interested in my own work, read *Winesburg, Ohio, Triumph of the Egg*, etc.

As suggested, I realize that the suggestions I am giving are not suggestions likely to lead you to any quick success, but they are the only kind of suggestions I feel able to make you. I am sorry that I cannot be of more definite help. Very truly yours

(P.S.) Stories returned under separate cover.

--Letter to Mrs. Harriet Martin, September 19, 1939, from *Letters of Sherwood Anderson*, #381

Once it was terribly important to me to be producing. Now it is just as important to me to be sitting here, writing to you, as it would be to write what they call a masterpiece. There is a kind of stillness in me. I should be scared. In the mood in which I have written this year I can sell little or nothing. I make no money. It doesn't bother me.

Sometimes I think I am reaching out for something. I don't know. I write and destroy, write and destroy. I don't care at all. I really feel healthy.

There is a way in which I do have to be a man of action too. It doesn't matter. It seems now almost as though I could become one and not at all lose the other thing. If it did not get expressed, what is the difference? It is like love. In a way you can keep loving.

--Letter to Charles Bockler, December 13, 1930, from *Letters of Sherwood Anderson,* #187

The arts are always being swept here and there by movements. It would be so satisfactory to us all if we could get the arts defined, if there were only some definite rule or formula by which, when we stand before a work of art, we could say "this is good or that is bad." Workmen in stone, in color, in sound, in words are always being bothered by the same desire. Mr. George Bellows must always have been on the hunt, trying one approach and then another. He died too soon. There are few enough such men.

My notion is that we would all chuck all of the arts out of our lives if we could. They are such a bother. The challenge is always there. "Get a little closer. Give more of yourself. Be more impersonal. Love more."

"Love what?"

Well, say this life in which we all live. That's something, isn't it? Life as it is in stones, trees, skies, seas, people, too.

Few enough people realize that all art that has vitality must have its basis in love.

--from *Sherwood Anderson's Notebook*, "After Seeing George Bellows' Mr. and Mrs. Wase"

Whether I'm any good or not, what I want is to work. The eternal quibbling about the purposes of art, its drift, etc., gets on my nerves, knocks me flat.

--Letter to Lucille Blum, July 1, 1923, from *Letters of Sherwood Anderson*, # 80

I float in many lives, am distressed, made gay, made happy—a thousand times each day.

What I have learned, a little, is not to try to express in words my understanding of moods I feel in others. People prefer such things kept secret.

The cook, a splendid brown girl with a strong body, has quarreled with her brown man. He got drunk and took money from her. The story is all told by the way she walks into a room. I keep silent, watching. After a time, if I am lucky, if my day is to be a fortunate one for me, I will escape into one life, one impulse, and get it working down through my fingers. To do that both exhausts and relieves me.

However I leave a trail behind. This man or woman I might have loved. There was a marvelous tale I might have told.

"Before my pen has gleaned my teeming brain."

Presently I shall die with a thousand, a hundred thousand tales untold. People I might have loved I shall not love.

As I stand in the bathroom preparing my body to receive others I am also preparing my mind. I came out of sleep a scattered thing, a sensitive plate ready to receive any sort of impression.

If my day is not to be a failure I must gather myself together and concentrate on one impression.

--from *Sherwood Anderson's Notebook*, "Notes Out of a Man's Life," Note 6

Early in June the tent will be set up, the waters of the lake shall lap on our shores, in the black hills fires will spring up where the iron mines lie, and we shall talk of the lands west of Chicago. Then I shall sing you my songs as the good old men sang. We shall sing and talk as old men talked before magazines and checks for stories came to corrupt their minds.

--Letter to Waldo Frank, ? May, 1917, from *Letters of Sherwood Anderson*, #13

I was in the country, having taken a room in the house of a certain family. There were many children. There was no place to work. There were young boys in the family.

There was a low shed, that had formerly, I believed, housed pigs. It had no doors or windows. It stood in the midst of a corn field.

The boys cleaned it and I helped. We shoveled dirt from the floor until we got down to the hard clean clay. We whitewashed the walls.

I moved my desk in there. I could not stand erect. While I worked in that place...again a madness of writing had seized me...the corn about me grew tall. The stalks pushed through the open windows, through the low doorway. A broad green corn leaf lay across the corner of my desk.

I wrote a book of childhood, an American childhood. It was in that place that a certain sentence came into my head. I was hoping that if, after my death, there were any who wished to do me honor they would honor me, not for what I had written, but for the full rich life I have lived. I was craving to be known as one man who had never saved, never provided for the morrow, as a man who wished only to live in the Now.

"Life, not Death, is the great adventure," I wrote.

For years I have been jotting down these impressions, memories, things seen and felt during what has continued to seem to me a very good life. On all sides now I hear complaints of the quality of life in our times. Possibly in years to come men will look back upon our time and speak of it as another dark age. Any civilization absorbed in economics, in war, in the economic interpretation of history, etc., can but be a savage and brutal civilization. It may be that I was born one of the lucky ones.

To be sure as a writer I have had endless miserable days. Black gloom having settled upon me often has stayed for days, weeks and months and these black times have always been connected with my work. I have been too eager. I have wanted to create constantly, never stopping. Yet what man at all sensitive to life doesn't have these weeks and months of gloom? And there have come these rich glad times. In a perhaps muddled time I have lived fully.

Has any man of my time approached me in richness of living? Perhaps Lawrence; but in my own experience of men I have never met another who has smelled, tasted, felt, seen as I have. I have been all my life a wanderer but my wandering has been to some purpose. America is a vast country. I have wanted to feel all of it in its thousand phases, see it, walk upon it—its plains, mountains, towns, cities, rivers, lakes, forests and plowed lands. I have been a true son of God in my eager love for and appreciation of nature. It is only through nature and art that men really live.

Women to me are related always to the world of nature, the male to the spirit. To me they have been, when not trying also to be male, the good earth. I am very male and do not believe in women artists—and these men feminists, how they bore me, how they make my bones ache with boredom. To me women are a flowing stream in which I bathe and clothe myself. They are rich wine drunk, fruit eaten. They have washed me as summer rains wash me. It is because I am so very male that I can be a real lover of women. But although I am essentially male I am not particularly lustful. There has been too much of the male energy in me gone into the effort to produce a beautiful art, to permit that. I have succeeded sometimes, failed often. But I believe in art. It is my only central purpose to produce, now and then, a flash of beauty in work. Not only because in the end nothing lives on but art.

The male desires not to be beautiful but to create beauty, and no woman can be beautiful without the help of the male. We create their beauty, fertilize it, feed it. In reality women have no desire to do. Doing is for them a substitute. Their desire is to BE. There was never a real woman lived who did not hunger to be beautiful. Woman is not man; I have had to write a book about this and it went unnoticed. If we were a strong race our women would be more beautiful, our land and our cities more beautiful. Because Americans have no understanding of women America has become a matriarchy.

All evil, all ugliness is a sign of weakness. The men in America who build ugly cities, ugly factory towns, who make fields and forests ugly, who make wars, cry out constantly the word progress, progress, to cover the fact of their ugly work—these are all weak men.

--from *Sherwood Anderson's Memoirs*, "Book VI, Life, Not Death—11. The Fortunate One"

I myself have had an unhappy year. I think often that a good many people, perhaps you, dear Brooks, among them, think of me as a mere reckless adventurer, but I have been up to something with my life and work. I am not a mere rudderless ship, and now and then I do make a port.

--Letter to Van Wyck Brooks, early October 1923, from *Letters of Sherwood Anderson*, #87

As for this book in hand, it's still on the knees of the gods, delicately balanced there between good and bad, perhaps. I should really have something to say. Stieglitz, Paul, Brooks, Frank, so many others have as a kind of gift so much I have struggled for, am still struggling for. I don't so much want to tell of anything accomplished as I want to tell the tale of a journey toward understanding of whatever may be beautiful and fine in life, my own life and other lives.

--Letter to Georgia O'Keeffe, August 4, 1923, from *Letters of Sherwood Anderson*, # 83

There is something very confusing to both readers and writers about the notion of realism in fiction. As generally understood it is akin to what is called "representation" in painting. The fact is before you and you put it down, adding a high spot here and there, to be sure. No man can quite make himself a camera. Even the most realistic worker pays some tribute to what is called "art." (Where does representation end and art begin?) The location of the line is often as confusing to practicing artists as it is to the public.

Recently a young writer came to talk with me about our mutual craft. He spoke with enthusiastic admiration of a certain book—very popular a year or two ago. "It is the very life. So closely observed. It is the sort of thing I should like to do. I should like to bring life itself within the pages of a book. If I could do that I would be happy."

I wondered. The book in question had only seemed to me good in spots and the spots had been far apart. There was too much dependence upon the notebook. The writer had seemed to me to have very little to give out of himself. What had happened, I thought, was that the writer of the book had confused the life of reality with the life of the fancy. Easy enough to get a thrill out of people with reality. A man struck by an automobile, a child falling out at the window of a city office building. Such things stir the emotions. No one, however, confuses them with art.

This confusion of the life of the imagination with the life of reality is a trap into which most of our critics seem to me to fall about a dozen times each year. Do the trick over and over and in they tumble. "It is life," they say. "Another great artist has been discovered."

What never seems to come quite clear is the simple fact that art is art. It is not life.

The life of the imagination will always remain separated from the life of reality. It feeds upon the life of reality, but it is not that life—cannot be. Mr. John Marin painting Brooklyn Bridge, Henry Fielding writing *Tom Jones*, are not trying in the novel and the painting to give us reality. They are striving for a realization in art of something out of their own imaginative experiences, fed to be sure upon the life immediately about. A quite different matter from making an actual picture of what they see before them.

And here arises a confusion. For some reason—I myself have never exactly understood very clearly—the imagination must constantly feed upon reality or starve. Separate yourself too much from life and you may at moments be a lyrical poet, but you are not an artist. Something within dries up, starves for the want of food. Upon the fact in nature the imagination must constantly feed in order that the imaginative life remains significant. The workman who lets his imagination drift off into some experience altogether disconnected with reality, the attempt of the American to depict life in Europe, the New Englander writing of cowboy life—all that sort of thing—in ninety-nine cases out of a hundred ends in the work of such a man becoming at once full of holes and bad spots. The intelligent reader, tricked often enough by the technical skill displayed in hiding the holes, never in the end accepts it as good work. The imagination of the workman has become confused. He has had to depend altogether upon tricks. The whole job is a fake.

The difficulty, I fancy, is that so few workmen in the arts will accept their own limitations. It is only when the limitation is fully accepted that it ceases to be a limitation. Such men scold at the life immediately about. "It's too dull and commonplace to make good material," they declare. Off they sail in fancy to the South Seas, to Africa, to China. What they cannot realize is their own dullness. Life is never dull except to the dull.

The writer who sets himself down to write a tale has undertaken something. He has undertaken to conduct his readers on a trip through the world of his fancy. If he is a novelist his imaginative world is filled with people and events. If he have any sense of decency as a workman he can no more tell lies about his imagined people, fake them, than he can sell out real people in real life. The thing is constantly done but no man I have ever met, having done such a trick, has felt very clean about the matter afterward.

On the other hand, when the writer is rather intensely true to the people of his imaginative world, when he has set them down truly, when he does not fake, another confusion arises. Being square with your people in the imaginative world does not mean lifting them over into life, into reality. There is a very subtle distinction to be made and upon the writer's ability to make this distinction will in the long run depend his standing as a workman.

Having lifted the reader out of the reality of daily life it is entirely possible for the writer to do his job so well that the imaginative life becomes to the reader for the time real life. Little real touches are added. The people of the town—that never existed except in the fancy—eat food, live in houses, suffer, have moments of happiness and die. To the writer, as he works, they are very real. The imaginative world in which he is for the time living has become for him more alive than the world of reality ever can become. His very sincerity confuses. Being unversed in the matter of making the delicate distinction, that the writer himself sometimes has such a hard time making, they call him a realist. The notion shocks him. "The deuce, I am nothing of the kind," he says. "But such a thing could not have happened in a Vermont town." "Why not? Have you not learned that anything can happen anywhere? If a thing can happen in my imaginative world it can of course happen in the flesh and blood world. Upon what do you fancy my imagination feeds?"

My own belief is that the writer with a notebook in his hand is always a bad workman, a man who distrusts his own imagination. Such a man describes actual scenes accurately, he puts down actual conversation.

But people do not converse in the book world as they do in life. Scenes of the imaginative world are not real scenes.

The life of reality is confused, disorderly, almost always without apparent purpose, whereas in the artist's imaginative life there is purpose. There is determination to give the tale, the song, the painting Form—to make it true and real to the theme, not to life. Often the better the job is done the greater the confusion.

I myself remember with what a shock I heard people say that one of my own books, *Winesburg, Ohio*, was an exact picture of Ohio village life. The book was written in a crowded tenement district of Chicago. The hint for almost every character was taken from my fellow lodgers in a large rooming house, many of whom had never lived in a village. The confusion arises out of the fact that others besides practicing artists have imaginations. But most people are afraid to trust their imaginations and the artist is not.

Would it not be better to have it understood that realism, in so far as the word means reality to life, is always bad art—although it may possibly be very good journalism?

Which is but another way of saying that all of the so-called great realists were not realists at all and never intended being. Madame Bovary did not exist in fact. She existed in the imaginative life of Flaubert and he managed to make her exist also in the imaginative life of his readers.

I have been writing a story. A man is walking in a street and suddenly turns out of the street into an alleyway. There he meets another man and a hurried whispered conversation takes place. In real life they may be but a pair of rather small bootleggers, but they are not that to me.

When I began writing, the physical aspect of one of the men, the one who walked in the street, was taken rather literally from life. He looked strikingly like a man I once knew, so much like him in fact that there was a confusion. A matter easy enough to correct.

A stroke of my pen saves me from realism. The man I knew in life had red hair; he was tall and thin.

With a few words I have changed him completely. Now he has black hair and a black mustache. He is short and has broad shoulders. And now he no longer lives in the world of reality. He is a denizen of my own imaginative world. He can now begin a life having nothing at all to do with the life of the red-haired man.

If I am to succeed in making him real in this new world he, like hundreds of other men and women who live only in my own fanciful world, must live and move within the scope of the story or novel into which I have cast him. If I do tricks with him in the imaginative world, sell him out, I become merely a romancer. If, however, I have the courage to let him really live he will, perhaps, show me the way to a fine story or novel.

But the story or novel will not be a picture of life. I will never have had any intention of making it that.

--from *Sherwood Anderson's Notebook*, "A Note on Realism"

...And what was the fear that had come upon me, the fear of old age, an old age of poverty?

But you will not starve. At the worst you will have more than your mother ever had during her whole life. You will wear better clothes, eat better food. You may be even able to retain this beautiful house a book of yours built.

I stood that night by my wife's bed, having this argument with myself, the whole matter being one that will interest only other artists, realizing dimly as I stood thus, that the fear in me that night, of which my wife knew nothing...it would have shocked her profoundly to be told of it...the fear perhaps came up into me from a long line of men and women...I remembered that night how my father, in his occasional sad moods...he was, most of the time rather a gay dog...used to go sit in the darkness of our house in a street of workingmen's houses, and sitting there, the rest of us suddenly silent, sing in a low voice a song called "Over the Hill to the Poor-House."

The fear in him too, perhaps into him from his father and his father's father and on back and back, all perhaps men who had lived as I had always lived, precariously.

It is what gets a man. In the artist there must always be this terrible contradiction. It is in all of us. We want passionately the luxuries of life, the things we produce—our books, paintings, statues, the songs we make, the music we make—these are all luxuries.

We want luxuries, for who but his fellow artists can really love the work of the artist while at the same time knowing, deep down in us, that if we give way to this passion for the possession of beautiful things about us, getting them by cheapening our own work, all understanding of beauty must go out of us.

--from *Sherwood Anderson's Memoirs*, 8. "Book V, Into the Thirties, The Sound of the Stream"

I have hurt so many people, Charles, trying to keep some integrity. Do I dare go on existing? A few tales, told at last. To push something out a little beyond the horizon, no one caring much.

The painter fighting, just for ground on which his easel may stand, the writer for his quiet room, his thoughts, word fitted against word as color.

--Letter to Charles Bockler, ? 1929, from *Letters of Sherwood Anderson*, #154

Don't quarrel with me if it suits my humor to let much go to hell while I try for a while to catch something of the song of men, machines, and the ground.

--Letter to Waldo Frank, ? May, 1917, from *Letters of Sherwood Anderson*, #14

I would like, if I could do it clearly and well, to say something definite to you about the artist's life.

I would like to see growth of that life here. I am writing to you this because you are a young man.

Charles* says that as yet, he is quite sure, you have too much regard left for established things. You believe yet that Yale is doing something and Harvard and the University of Chicago.

You believe the great cities are building to some purpose, that wars are fought for a purpose, nations established so.

It is not so, my dear man.

There is no purpose other than the artist's purpose and the purpose of the woman. The artist purposes to bring to life, out of the-- of hidden form in lives, nature, things, the living form as women purpose doing that out of their lovely bodies.

The artist there is your only true male, and for those formed male it is the only life with purpose in it.

If a man does not have the courage to propose to himself to attempt living that life, let him at least be humble before it.

Why, I myself have be(en) accused of being a morally loose man. It is said I have made physical love to many women.

I have made physical love to but few. Any common rake in this town could outdo me at that.

In truth I have made love to whole armies of women.

When I saw you in New York, I said a little to you about the artist's life. I would like to see artists in America become a bit more class-conscious. I would like to see them become men of pride in their bearing.

I would like to see them quit kneeling down before money and middle-class moral standards.

There must come someday real morality here. Towns must be comprehended, lives, fields, rivers, mountains, cities.

--Letter to Dwight MacDonald, ? April, 1929, from *Letters of Sherwood Anderson*, #158

*Charles Bockler

There has been, for a long time now, and with America and Germany as the most outstanding leaders of the movement, a tremendous standardization of life going on in every country of the western world.

As an example of what I am trying to get at, let me start by restating a fact, well known to every American past forty, the obvious fact that within our own day there has come a great change in the mechanics of the everyday life of every American man, woman, and child.

There have been these two things—the speeding up and the standardization of life and thought, the one impulse no doubt the result of the other.

In my own father's day, for example, there was not a man of our Ohio town, counting himself at all a person of intelligence, who did not know the name of the editor of every outstanding New York, Chicago, Cincinnati or New Orleans newspaper. Not only the names but the personalities and dominant characteristics of many of these editors were known to men within the radius of the territories in which their newspapers circulated, and often far outside. The entire daily press of the country was dominated by men of strong individuality who were continually making a direct and powerful appeal out of their own complex minds to readers all over the country.

You have but to compare the city newspaper of today with that of a generation ago to get a quite startling realization of what has happened. In the newspaper world now are there any such towering figures as our fathers knew? If there are, who are they?

When it comes to that, does the average citizen of any American city today know or care who is editor of the newspaper he reads in the morning? A man doesn't think of personalities in connection with newspapers any more. The passing from active service of Colonel Henry Watterson, of the Louisville *Courier-Journal*, saw pass also the last of the old type of unique individuals impressing their personalities on people in general through the ownership or editorship of newspapers. Chicago, a city of the gods know how many hundred thousands nameless human beings drifting daily through crowded, noise-haunted streets, in and out of the doors of apartment and office buildings, department stores and factories, has two morning newspapers, printed in English.

Paris, a city half the size of Chicago, has some thirty French daily newspapers.

And Paris, you will remember, is inhabited by one people while Chicago has within its limits a conglomeration of peoples from all over the world, newly come together and trying to make of themselves one people—a new people—the Americans of the future.

There is something very amazing indicated by all this.

In one city the attempt is being made to channel the minds of all men into one iron groove while in the other the idiosyncrasies of individuals and groups are given breathing space and many channels of expression. The impulse has its roots in the somewhat strange notion, that has for a long time been becoming more and more prevalent among us, a notion that to conform to type is man's highest mission.

A rather strange doctrine, that, to be so universally accepted in the "land of the free and the home of the brave?"

--from *Sherwood Anderson's Notebook*, "Notes on Standardization"

I would so like to write, before I die, one joyous book, not at all sentimentally joyous, but having in it a deeper joy...You do have to fight so for this elusive joy—just why, in our civilization, I don't know.

--Letter to Mr. And Mrs. B.E. Copenhaver and May Scherer, early January, 1934, from *Letters of Sherwood Anderson*, #242

...As happens sometimes when I publish a new book, strange, lonely, defeated people write to me. They want—love, I fancy. "You will understand my need," they say.

It opens wide fields. One can't come close to so many. You know, I fancy. One has to save some strength for work, hoping that out of it a little beauty and meaning may come. One can't be a preacher or an evangelist.

--Letter to Alfred Stieglitz and Georgia O'Keeffe,
December 7, 1923, from *Letters of Sherwood Anderson*, # 91

I rather fancied you might like *Many Marriages*. Perhaps I'm getting a little better hold of the longer form. That is what I have wanted. To get the longer form well in hand and then pour the tale into it as wine in a vessel. We'll see. It's job enough, God knows, to keep me at work the rest of my life.

--Letter to Georgia O'Keeffe, August 4, 1923, from *Letters of Sherwood Anderson*, #83

...and I suppose that is what every artist wants—to leave thus living traces of the fine thing in himself for other craftsmen to see and understand a little.

--Letter to Alfred Stieglitz, June 30, 1923, from *Letters of Sherwood Anderson*, #79

...In conversation he was wonderful. He came into my room and sat. He spoke of his youth, told stories of his childhood, of his courting of his wife. There was in all his talk a curious naive honesty and I listened, filled with joy. He had, in conversation, a way of suddenly dropping a sentence that illuminated perfectly the scene or person he was describing and as he talked thus my own fingers itched to get a pen in my hand. It may be that my affection for him was largely due to this. He was a feeder. He fed me. Often, after an hour with him in my room, I put aside the story I was working on to put down his story just as he told it. Some of the best stories I ever wrote I got from him thus, using often his very language. Once or twice, when he had told me one of his stories I sent him off to his own room.

"Now go and write that story just as you have told it to me," I said and he tried.

It never came off. With the pen in his hand he became again the "newspaper Ned."

What cliches, what flatness. I grew unscrupulous. I let him feed me. I used him. In my life I have known several such people, feeders to others. Their talk is wonderful. There are sentences dropped into their talk that make you want to shout with joy. With pen in hand they become self-conscious.

"Now I am writing."

It may be they are conscious of a possible audience for what they write. What is in them will not flow down their arms and into their fingers. The pen in their hands kills for them all spontaneity, all free expression.

Annoying things were always happening to my friend and how well he told of them.

He had an affair with a woman somewhat older than himself. She was living with her father and mother in a house on the East Side. This was when he had a room near my own.

He used to go to her, perhaps twice a month. Her father and mother, he told me, were quite old. "So I go there. If they have gone to bed, the window shade of her room is fixed in just a certain way. The front door of the house has been left unlocked. She has crept down and unlocked it.

"So I go up. I have taken off my shoes. I go up softly and there, I am in her arms."

It was hard to imagine my friend in a woman's arms. He was so big and awkward, so like a huge bear, but there he was. He had loved the woman for a long time and there was something sad about the story. From all he told me she must have been a very gentle one, a contrast no doubt to his wife. She believed in his writing.

"She thinks I am a genius," he once said to me, smiling sadly. For all of his continuing to write he was always sharply aware of his own deficiencies.

"I'll never make it, but what do I care? It gives me great satisfaction," he once said to me.

It was a winter night and snowing, and being restless in his little cramped room he had gone to his love. He had already told me that she had a weak heart.

He had gone there at perhaps two in the morning. He crept up to her. In the ecstasy of love she died in his arms.

He must have been horribly frightened.

"So I arranged everything in the room and then I crept out," he said.

He was on the stairs of the house and the stairs creaked. He did not know whether in creeping away thus he was trying to protect himself or her. She had always, he said, been what is called a good woman. No breath of scandal had ever touched her. "I wanted her old father and mother to find her there, thinking her innocent as they had always thought of her," he said.

He got out of the house and into the street. It was snowing and there was a heavy fall of snow on the ground. With his shoes in his hand he ran. He ran through the street. There was a kind of wild ecstasy of running. He stumbled and fell. He got up and ran again. In some way he got through Central Park and to the West Side unnoticed.

"Once I was noticed," he later told me. Some men shouted at him but he dodged into a side path and kept running.

He arrived in my room (it might have been three in the morning) with his shoes still clutched in his hand. He lay on the floor and sobbed. It was one of the strange sort of things that were always happening to him.

His whole life, as I knew it and as he told it to me, was filled with strange, sometimes terrible adventures but he did not write of them.

I had a letter from him this morning. No doubt as I write this he is sitting somewhere in a room writing. He has started another novel. He has read a novel, let us say, by H.G. Wells. He tries his hand at one rather like that. His writing will still be flat and rather meaningless. It will be full of newspaper cliches. Strange, amusing and sometimes terrible things will still be happening to him but he cannot really tell of them except in talk.

It is his fate. He is not a writer. He is one who feeds writers. There are a good many such in the world.

--from *Sherwood Anderson's Memoirs*, "Book V, Into the Thirties, 7. The Feeders"

... I dare say that my experience with manuscripts is that of most writers. For a good many years it never occurred to me that anyone would want the sheets on which I have scrawled. Naturally I threw them all in the wastepaper basket. Occasionally one does show up. I write both on the typewriter and in longhand. I have certainly never offered my manuscripts for sale. When I discovered that they seem to have some value to some people, that is to say, to collectors, I presented all of them that I could find to a personal friend who happens to be a collector. I do not believe he would want me to give his name. He is a collector and has money, and other writers might get after him. I would myself if I were broke and found I could get money for these discarded sheets.

Yes, of course I am bothered by collectors. What writer isn't?

I never could find myself much flattered by all this. I have always felt that the so-called admirers of a certain writer who wanted one of his manuscripts was a good deal like a lover who wanted one of his lady's old dresses instead of the lady herself. Surely what there is of a writer should be in his work.

--Letter to Mr. Fred Wittner, *New York Herald Tribune*, January 2, 1935, from *Letters of Sherwood Anderson*, #254

Dear Carrow De Vries: That was a very fine letter. The very instant you speak of, the woman remembering a scene in the kitchen, is the whole end a man is working for.

Light in darkness.

Your own scene in the drugstore, holding the pencil and pad of paper, arises to what seems a kind of glorious clearness.

You write so freely of this scene, so that I see you, the man in the store, the street outside. To make me see something so vividly, the intensity of life in you at the moment, makes new life in me. So that I am for the moment no longer blind.

Isn't that the object of all so-called art?

How many such moments can we crowd into a life? So much of life being so dark.

We are such curiously lonely creatures.

Such flashes open doors, but I think that when you wrote to me of the scene in the drugstore, you did not quite know it was then you were writing well. It may have been because you had forgotten you were writing and were thinking only of the moment. Sincerely

--Letter to Carrow De Vries, October 5, 1939, from
Letters of Sherwood Anderson, #382

Chapter Two

The Process
How does writing happen?

A book or story, when you are writing it, must get to the place where reading what you have already written excites you to write more.

If you come to a day when you cannot write, do not try. If you force yourself what you write at such times will poison all the future pages. If you do write at such times throw all away.

Every writer should say to himself every morning, "I do not have to write. I can be a tramp."

When a story gets to the place where reading over what you have written excites you to write more it has done what I call "come alive."

It will go now if you let it. Be patient. Go talk to men. Go fishing or swimming. When your fingers itch run home to your desk and write again.

I write down rules like this because I break them so often and when I do break them I feel such a fool.

--from *Sherwood Anderson's Notebook*, "Notes Out of a Man's Life," Note 3

No, dear reader, my aim in this book is to tell another sort of story, the story of a mind groping, in the end perhaps reaching expression in an art, of what then happens to the work of art itself, how in its turn must grope, trying to find its own life.

--from *Sherwood Anderson's Memoirs*, "Book I, What A Man's Made Of, 7. New Worlds"

Dear Brother: Here is a notion that can't fail to interest you. I am proposing to write a book to be called *Industrial Vistas**. It is to be the autobiography of a man's secondary self, of the queer, unnamed fancies that float through his brain, the things that appear to have no connection with actualities.

In me, and, I fancy, in most men, odd, detached fancies are born, blossom, sometimes like flowers, sometimes like evil-seeming weeds, then appear to pass.

My notion is that no man knows himself or can arrive at truth concerning himself except by what seems like indirection. I have a desire to take hold of indirection as a tool and use it in an attempt to arrive at truth.

--Letter to Trigant Burrow, ? October, 1919, from *Letters of Sherwood Anderson*, #42

*Not published

Dear Brother: I have come to think of the muddle of life as a necessary thing and all direct effort at corrective measures as rather absurd. Perhaps the muddle is a fertilizing thing like the stable manure thrown on the fields.

--Letter to Waldo Frank, late December, 1917, from *Letters of Sherwood Anderson*, #26

...Still as fast as I wrote, I threw away. On other occasions a kind of sickness overcame me. For a week or two I would do no work. I would destroy bales of my writing, walk restlessly about at night, get myself drunk. It seemed to me that these hundreds of thousands of words put down amounted to nothing, that I was merely aping the writings of other men I had read, that I had no clear and honest outlook on life and was utterly incapable of getting one. I must say that in all the writing I had done up to this time there was little or no originality. I was the "sedulous ape," continually reading novels—but not, as was afterwards said, the Russians, whom I read only long after I was accused of imitating them. I was under the spell of the earlier novels of H.G. Wells, and those of Thomas Hardy, Arnold Bennett and George Moore. Of George Borrow I had long been a devotee, and like most young men who have a leaning toward literature I read and reread George Moore's *Confessions of a Young Man.* How I longed to be such another, to live in some city like Paris, the center of the art expression of a nation, to have beautiful mistresses, to have an estate in Ireland as Moore had, from which I would get sufficient money to sustain me in the life I loved. I would not of course have objected if the money had come from an estate in Iowa or Kansas.

But beautiful mistresses did not flock to me...During these periods all the ugliness of my quarters came more and more into my consciousness. At such times I did not want to return to my rooms...

I would return to my rooms and sit at my desk and write. My life had become an absurdity. But perhaps I could bury myself in other, imagined lives. Words poured out of me. Often it did not work. The pencil dropped from my fingers and I sat at my desk, staring out at the window. I seemed to myself altogether alone in the world.

I turned to look at the pile of manuscript on my desk. "Why am I doing this?" I asked myself. "I have so and so many hundreds of thousands of words, but why?" Nothing I had written seemed to have any life. Could I make my stories live? Would I ever achieve that wonder? "If I could do that I would not be so lonely," I kept telling myself. I could surround myself with imagined figures so real that they would be like companions to me.

There was something I constantly sought. What was it? It seemed to me that most of all I wanted to lose self. There was a constant feeling of dirt within. "I have made myself filthy," I told myself. I think it was this feeling of dirt in life, in myself, that had destroyed my relations with my family. I had children but did not live with my family. I kept trying to think my way through my own muddle. It was at about this time that the woman suffrage movement reached its peak. Some of the women in the office where I worked were in the movement.

I did not believe in it. They would get the vote, but what of it? Basically men and women were not alike. I tried to think my way through this problem. "A woman can exist fully in a physical world. She can create in a physical world. Children come out of her body." Often at this time I half wished I was myself a woman. I would go get a lover, would have many children.

But I, a male, was striving to have children in another world and they would not emerge. I threw my pencil down, walked out of my room into the street. Often I went along muttering to myself. "The male world is the world of the spirit," I told myself. All of my pronouncements were, to be sure, constantly being refuted by women artists but they were very dear to me. I had wanted in myself a kind of great tenderness toward all life but the dirt within kept making me more and more disagreeable with others.

"I cannot go on in this way," I kept telling myself. The mood I was in at this time led to a sort of nervous breakdown. I was still strong, could at times work in the office all day and coming home write all night, without a sense of weariness, but I had a disease. It was the disease of self. I knew that. Perhaps I could escape out of myself into the life of some woman. I began creating a new dream, that of becoming a great lover, the lover of any number of beautiful women.

It was early summer and I left my room. I was unable to work, and went along Fifty-seventh Street to the park. I walked restlessly about. "I will go get myself a woman, will lose myself in her." The dreams of having women were as absurd as the other dreams I was having. What did I expect? I half expected some beautiful woman to stop me on the paths. "I want you. You are very beautiful to me. Come with me. Come into my arms." Did I expect something of this kind to happen? Really, I didn't in a real world, but in the world of the dream it could happen. I constantly passed couples walking together. There was a very beautiful young woman, elegantly dressed, who walked with a very dignified, gray-haired man. He was, I had no doubt, her father.

I began to follow them. They strolled through the Park and went to walk by the lake and I was at their heels. It was a wonder I was not arrested. They went to sit on the stone steps of the Field Museum. They were on the side of the building that looked out over a small lagoon and were engaged in low-voiced conversation. There was no one else near and I went to sit near them. I kept looking at the woman. How beautiful she was. Why did she not speak to me? Why did she not leave the older man, her father, and come to me? "I am not physically unattractive. I have a mind. I have an imagination. I am a poet." These sentences I whispered to myself. I grew suddenly ashamed and getting up crept away. There had been a pause in the conversation of the man and the woman. The man had noticed me hanging about. "Who is that fellow? He has been following us. Do you know the fellow?" I did not hear his words but in some inner way knew they had been spoken. I crept away like a thief.

A strange sort of fear took possession of me. Sometimes I wandered about half the night in the streets. There was an outbreak of holdups in Chicago at the time and twice I became a victim, once losing my watch and some small change and at another time a roll of bills containing $20 or $30. In the state I was in, the holdups did not frighten me. I tried to laugh and joke with one of the holdup men, but he cut me short. He gave me to understand that business with him was business.

"Shut your trap or I'll plug you," was what he said.

The depression continued for months. I could not come out of it. Occasionally I picked up some woman of the streets, tried to get comfort from association with her. It did not work, and after such experiences I fell into deeper gloom. I went about alone and into the lower class of saloons. Tried to get into some sort of relation with men and women picked up in such places. There must have been at the time in me some notion that if I could find people sufficiently low in the social scale, I would find comrades. Myself I felt to be an utterly defeated man and wanted others who were defeated. I drank a good deal and went muttering through the streets. I carried a little note-book in my pocket and sitting at some beer-stained table in a low saloon, wrote sentences.

"It is only when you are defeated and drift like a rudderless ship that I can come close to you," I wrote.

During this deep depression, a mood that everyone working in the arts, particularly in America, must know, I had a rather strange experience. It may be that I was for the time slightly insane. I had left the advertising office at noon, had gone out to lunch and found myself unable to return. I took a street car and went south to my old quarters, but could not stay there. I went to walk in Jackson Park.

49

There was in the Park a small island that during the Chicago World's Fair had been known as the Japanese Village. It was approached by beautiful little bridges built by the Japanese, and I went there to sit. I had brought from my room a thick tablet of paper. At that time I had always the feeling that at any moment I might begin to really write. There would be some response out of my very self to the life about me.

"Somewhere within me there must be sleeping a true man," I kept saying to myself.

I was sitting on a bench beside a path on the island in the park and people kept passing up and down before me. There were young men and old men, young women and old women. A pair of lovers came and sat on a nearby bench, but were soon embarrassed by my presence. They went away. At the moment none of them seemed real to me. The tree under which I sat, the grass in the Park, the water in the nearby lagoon, the beautiful little Japanese bridges, none of these things seemed real. I remember that I leaned forward on the bench and touched the gravel path with my fingers.

"It is real. This is the earth. These are little stones I hold here in my hand," I muttered to myself.

There were a young man and woman passing and I began suddenly to laugh.

"I have gone a little crazy," I told myself, but I did not care. "How do I know these are little stones I hold in my hand? They may be rare and precious jewels," I said aloud.

The young man and woman paused and stared at me. A look of fear came into the eyes of the woman. The man and woman were whispering together.

"You do not need to be afraid. You are quite beautiful. No woman who is beautiful needs to be afraid," I said.

Turning occasionally to stare back at me, the young man and woman hurried away.

Left alone on the bench beside the path on the little island in the Park, I suddenly began to write. I wrote rapidly, with a kind of insane abandon. Hours passed and I continued writing. It seemed to me that I wrote a thousand, ten thousand, a hundred thousand words. At last I wrote a long and completely beautiful story. Oh, with what precision the words were laid against each other. The words had become like beautiful jewels to me. How tender I was with them, how skillful my fingers, how superlatively skillful my brain.

The truth is, of course, that I was exhausted when I went there and what had really happened was that I had sat down on the bench and gone to sleep. All of the things that I have put down here as having happened, my feeling the earth with my fingers, my speaking to the young woman accompanied by the man, all of this took place in a dream.

But the strange part of the experience was that the dream seemed to continue when I awoke. I did not look at the tablet I held in my hand, so convinced was I that I had written a beautiful story. I walked home to my room and laid the tablet on the table, went out to a restaurant and dined and returning to my room, undressed and went to bed. I was happy and relaxed and fell at once into a long and dreamless sleep. I did not awaken until morning and my awakening brought a strange shock to me. For a time I lay in the bed, still convinced that I had at last written a beautiful story and then, getting out of bed, I went, filled with hope and fear, to the table where I had laid the tablet. The tablet, of course, was blank.

--from *Sherwood Anderson's Memoirs*, "Book III, A Robin's Egg Renaissance, 3. In Jackson Park"

I have seldom written a story, long or short, that I did not have to write and rewrite. There are single short stories of mine that have taken me ten or twelve years to get written. It isn't that I have lingered over sentences, being one of the sort of writers who say... "Oh, to write the perfect sentence." It is true that Gertrude Stein once declared I was one of the few American writers who could write a sentence. Very well. I am always pleased with any sort of flattery. I love it. I eat it up. For years I have had my wife go over all criticisms of my work. "I can make myself miserable enough," I have said to her. "I do not want others to make me miserable about my work." I have asked her to show me only the more favorable criticisms. There are enough days of misery, of black gloom.

However this has leaked through to me. There is the general notion, among those who make a business of literary criticism and who have done me the honor to follow me more or less closely in my efforts, that I am best at the short story.

And I do not refer here to those who constantly come to me saying, "*Winesburg* contains your best work," and who, when questioned, admit they have never read anything else. I refer instead to the opinion that is no doubt sound.

The short story is the result of sudden passion. It is an idea grasped whole as one would pick an apple in an orchard. All of my own short stories have been written at one sitting, many of them under strange enough circumstances There are these glorious moments, these pregnant hours and I remember such hours as a man remembers the first kiss got from a woman loved.

I was in the little town of Harrodsburg in Kentucky...this when I was still a writer of advertisements. It was evening and I was at a railroad station—a tiny station as I remember it and all day had been writing advertisements of farm implements. A hunch had come to me and I had bought a yellow tablet of paper at a drug store as I walked to the station. I began writing on a truck on the station platform...I stood by the truck writing. There were men standing about and they stared at me.

It did not matter. The great passion had come upon me and the men standing about, small town men, loitering about the station, now and then walking past me...the train must have been late but it was a summer night and the light lasted...

There were crates of live chickens at the other end of the truck on which I rested my tablet. There is this curious absorption that at the same time permits a great awareness.

You are, as you are not at other times, aware of all going on about you, of the color and shapes of the clouds in the sky, of happenings along a street, of people passing, the expression of faces, clothes people wear...all of your senses curiously awake...

At the same time an intense concentration on the matter in hand. Oh that I could live all of my life so. Once I wrote a poem about a strange land few of us ever enter. I called it the land of the Now.

How rapidly they march. How the words and sentences flow, how they march.

It is strange, but, now that I try to remember which of my stories I began, standing by the truck at the little railroad station at Harrodsburg, Kentucky, and finished riding in the day coach of the train on my way to Louisville, I can remember only the station, each board of the station wall, the places where the boards of the station wall had pulled loose, nails pulled half out. The tail feather of a rooster stuck out of one of the crates. Once later I made love to a woman in the moonlight in a field. We had gone into the field for that purpose. There were some white flowers, field daisies, and she plucked one of them. "I am going to keep it to remember this moment," she said.

So also did I pluck a feather from the tail of a rooster at the railroad station at Harrodsburg. I put it in my hat. "I will wear it for this moment, for the glorious peep I am having into the land of Now," I said to myself.

--from *Sherwood Anderson's Memoirs*, "Book IV, The Literary Life, 8. Writing Stories"

...I was a money-getter, a schemer, a chronic liar. One day I found out that when I sat down to write, it was more difficult to lie. The lie lay before one on the paper. It haunted one at night.

Then, you see, I knew no writers, no artists. Everything was very much mixed up. When I began to know writers and painters, I couldn't abide the way most of them talked. They were also doing the American trick. They were putting it over.

You see, I had by this time got up out of the ranks of laborers and lived among businessmen, had them for my friends. I went to conferences, lunched with these men. They were always talking so earnestly about nothing. The nothingness back of the spirit of their lives led to sex-mussiness. Brooks, I believe, once called me "the phallic Chekhov." I really do not believe I have a sex-obsession, as has so often been said. I do not want to have, surely. When I want to flatter myself, at least, I tell myself that I want only not to lose the sense of life as it is, here, now, in the land and among the people among whom I live.

--Letter to Paul Rosenfeld, after October 24, 1921, from *Letters of Sherwood Anderson*, #63

54

Dear Roy Jansen*: I think the most absorbingly interesting and exciting moment in any writer's life must come at the moment when he, for the first time, knows that he is a real writer. Any professional writer, any Hemingway, Wolfe, Faulkner, Stein, Dreiser, Lewis—I could name a dozen others, prosemen, I mean—will know what I mean. You begin, of course, being not yourself. We all do. There have been so many great ones. "If I could write as that man does." There is, more than likely, some one man you follow slavishly. How magnificently his sentences march. It is like a field being plowed. You are thinking of the man's style, his way of handling words and sentences.

You read everything the man has written, go from him to others. You read, read, read. You live in the world of books. It is only after a long time that you know that this is a special world, fed out of the world of reality, but not of the world of reality.

You have yourself not yet brought anything up out of the real world into this special world, to make it live there.

And then, if you are ever to be a real writer, your moment comes. I remember mine. I walked along a city street in the snow. I was working at work I hated. Already I had written several long novels. They were not really mine. I was ill, discouraged, broke. I was living in a cheap rooming house. I remember that I went upstairs and into the room. It was very shabby. I had no relatives in the city and few enough friends. I remember how cold the room was. On that afternoon I had heard that I was to lose my job.

I grew desperate, went and threw up a window. I sat by the open window. It began to snow. "I'll catch cold siting here."

"What do I care?" There was some paper on a small kitchen table I had bought and had brought up into the room. I turned on a light and began to write. I wrote, without looking up—I never changed a word of it afterwards—a story called "Hands." It was and is a very beautiful story.

I wrote the story and then got up from the table at which I had been sitting, I do not know how long, and went down into the city street. I thought that the snow had suddenly made the city very beautiful. There were people in the street, all sorts of people, shabby ones, brisk young ones, old discouraged ones. I went along wanting to hug people, to shout.

"I've done it. At last, after all of these years I've done something." How did I know I had? I did know. I was drunk with a new drunkenness. I cannot remember all of the absurd, foolish things I did that evening.

*Author and proprietor of a bookstore in Pittsburgh

I had a little money in my pocket and went into saloons. I called men up to the bar. "Drink. Drink to me, men." I remember that a prostitute accosted me and that I threw some money toward her and ran away laughing. It must have been several hours before I got the courage to return to my room and read my own story.

It was all right. It was sound. It was real. I went to sit by my desk. A great many others have had such moments. I wonder what they did. I sat there and cried. For the moment I thought the world very wonderful, and I thought also that there was a great deal of wonder in me.

--Letter to Roy Jansen, ? late April, 1935, from *Letters of Sherwood Anderson*, #260

I wrote the first of the stories, afterwards to be known as the Winesburg stories. I wrote it, as I wrote them all, complete in one sitting. I do not think I afterwards changed a word of it. I wrote it off so, sitting at my desk, in that room, the rain blowing in on me and wetting my back and when I had written it I got up from my desk.

The rest of the stories in the book came out of me on succeeding evenings, and sometimes during the day while I worked in the advertising office. At intervals there would be a blank space of a week, and then there would be two or three written during a week. I was like a woman having my babies, one after another but without pain.

--from *Sherwood Anderson's Memoirs*, "Book IV, The Literary Life, 1. Waiting for Ben Huebsch"

The typewriter is O.K. I merely work faster with the pen because I have never become expert on the machine.

--Letter to Laura Lou Copenhaver, November 9, 1937, from *Letters of Sherwood Anderson*, #327

Monte, I don't know what to say about the things you have sent. I am no critic. It seems fragmentary to me. You are having thoughts about the stars, the way the earth moves, have read Fabre and Jeans*. You seem, my dear, a bit awestruck by your own thoughts. I am afraid you are writing sentences. The sentence should fairly tear itself out of you because it must. It is, it seems to me, a terrible mistake to think in sentences.

To be sure I have got, from these fragments, little enough sense of your journey. You seem, Monte, to be floating off somewhere in the air. Didn't you ever have a bellyache or headache or an ingrowing toenail? It is so rarified. A man want(s) the smells, lusts, hurts, annoyances, surprises of strange places, and intimacy, self-revelation. You get so far away, in the stars, the moon, the moving earth.

No, I don't believe you have got to writing yet. If you do it, you'll have to get more in it, more of your own smallnesses, bignesses, secret lusts, a lot of stuff that will make it all less floating. Is this severe? Forgive me. I don't know what else to say.

Indeed I hope we may see you. We should be along in early November. Then you may pummel me, scorn me, spit at me.

But no great thought(s), Monte dear, no great thoughts.

What (a) bastard I am to speak so.

Do remember me to your father.

Love to you both.

--Letter to Margaret Bartlett, October, 1939, from *Letters of Sherwood Anderson*, #383

(Margaret Bartlett was one of the daughters of Judge George A. Bartlett of Reno who had presided over the case when Sherwood obtained his divorce from Tennessee Mitchell Anderson in 1924. She had sent Anderson the manuscript of a travel book which she had completed.)

*Presumably *The Heavens* by J.H. Fabre, translated by E.E.Fournier d'Albe, Philadelphia, 1925; and *Man and the Stars* by Sir James H. Jeans, New York, 1931. Miss Bartlett's book was dedicated to Jeans and Rainer Maria Rilke.

The relation between the artist and the workman is very subtle and difficult to define. Some artists feel it, others do not. There are artists who would like to deny it. They would like to think of themselves as aristocrats.

What a notion! The artist must work with his hands. He must feel within himself some deep relationship between himself, as a man, and the world of nature, of materials.

The earth in which men have always plowed and planted, trees, stones lying in fields, seas breaking on shores, a world filled with materials out of which he is to try to create something with his hands.

Workingmen also express themselves through their hands. Look at the hands of Mr. and Mrs. Wase. Years of touching things, doing things. The fingers, in the end, often become more alive than all the rest of the body...

--from *Sherwood Anderson's Notebook*, "After Seeing George Bellows' Mr. and Mrs. Wase"

I do not know whether or not, when you were at my place, you took much note of the man who runs my farm and who, with his son, was building the barn. He is a simple countryman and can barely read and write, but I must say gives me more satisfaction as a companion and friend than most of the artists who come to me and who are so terribly concerned about their genius and their missions.

Frankly, I do not believe this sort of thing concerns me at all. I have no feeling of being a public figure and do not want to be one, and often I think that my own interest in the lives of people about me has at bottom more integrity than this ambitious effort to think of masses of people, where they are going and what is best for them...

However, alas, I have no solution to offer. I think most people in life are pretty lonely. I think there is a tendency to live on this loneliness, make it something precious and personal.

You speak of this man, and you have talked to me a great deal of what Art means to you. You come to me and to Dreiser. I do not think we can really help. The truth is that we are probably wanting what you say you want, but have had experience enough to know that few men get it. I really think there is some danger of surrender to self-pity and also perhaps too much clutching at others. There is too much emphasis on what you can get from others and not enough on giving. This may sound like preaching, but it is pretty sound.

The truth is all I can see for you, if you play fair, is to return to Antioch and face your problem there.

I am sorry not to be more helpful. I do not know what else to say.

As always

--Letter to Mr. Gilbert Wilson, October 26, 1939, from *Letters of Sherwood Anderson*, #384

On that night I walked down the hill past my house and to a bridge over a stream and stood still arguing with myself.

"But I have a right now to put money first. I have got to begin now thinking of money. I have got to begin making money. I will—I will. These people of my story shall behave as I wish. For years I have been a slave to these people of my imagination but I will be a slave no longer. For years I have served them and now they shall serve me."

Here I was, standing in silence on the bridge over a stream...And there again were the sounds in the stream. They crept into me, invaded me. I heard again the sound of the feet of children, horses galloping, soldiers marching, the sob of that crippled girl. I heard the voices of old friends. The sounds went on for a time. Of a sudden the sounds all changed.

There were no more voices, only laughter. The laughter began. It increased in volume. It seemed to become a roar.

"See, the very stream is laughing at me," I cried and began to run along the country road that goes past my house. I ran and ran. I ran until I was exhausted. I ran up hill and down. I hurt my bare feet. I had come out of my house wearing bedroom slippers but I had lost them. I ran until I was out of breath, exhausted. I had hurt one of my feet on a sharp stone. It bled. I stopped running that night at the brow of a low hill, after all not far from my house...a man of my age, who has spent so much of his life at a desk, who has smoked so many hundreds of thousands, it may be near millions, of cigarettes, does not run far.

I ran until I was exhausted and then, hobbling along, as once a crippled girl in Chicago had hobbled sobbing beside me in a rain swept Chicago street, I went back over the road along which I had been running and to my cabin by the creek.

I let myself into my cabin and getting the manuscript on which I had been at work I took it out to a little open grassy place beside the stream and sitting there on the grass I burned it page by page.

The burning took a long time and it was a job. It was, I knew, an absurd performance; and I knew that I was, as all such men as myself must ever be, a child. But later, as you see, I have wanted to write of it, to see if in words I can catch the mood of it.

"It will be a joy to other writers, other artists, to know that I also, a veteran among them, am also as they are, a child," I thought.

I did all of this—as I have set it down, going at great length, as you will see, to catch the mood of it, to give it background—and then, being very careful with my cut foot, I went back to my house and to my bed.

However I went first to the bathroom. I put disinfectant on the cut on my foot and my wife awoke.

"What are you doing?" she asked me, speaking sleepily, and, "Oh, I just got up to go to the bathroom," I said. And so she slept again and before again getting into bed I stood for a time looking at her asleep.

"I dare say that all men, artists and others, are as I am, children, at bottom," I thought; and I wondered a little if it were true that only a few women among all the millions of women got, by the pain of living with us, a little mature.

I was again in my bed and I thought that the voices in the stream by my house had stopped laughing at me and that again they talked and whispered to me; and on the next morning my shoe hurt my foot so that, when I was out of my wife's sight, I hobbled painfully along. I went to my cabin and to the black spot on the grass by the creek where I had burned the attempt I had made to impose my own will on the people of my imaginative world. I began to laugh at myself.

It had, I thought, been an absurd and silly experience through which I had passed but, God knows, I told myself I may have to pass through it again, time after time. I knew as I sat down at my desk that morning, determined again not to impose myself, to let the story I was trying to write write itself, to be again what I had always been, a slave to the people of my imaginary world if they would do it, making their own story of their own loves, my pen merely forming the words on the paper...I knew that what I had been through, in such an absurd and childish form, letting myself again be a victim to old fears, was nevertheless the story of like experiences in the life of all artists, no doubt throughout time.

--from *Sherwood Anderson's Memoirs*, "Book V, Into The Thirties, 8. The Sound of the Stream"

Dear Carrow De Vries: I think looseness is but a part of it. The free flow wanted comes, I've a notion, from unconsciousness of the act of writing.

It is true that as a man walks along a street or sits, often with friends, he hears bits of conversations or the sounds of the street, while at the same time his thoughts go wandering, doing many strange things.

A certain amount of control is, of course, possible, or there would be no work done at all.

You sit with a group of people, and there is a conversation going on, words and sentences being made. At the same time there is an unspoken conversation. A man may be in such a group speaking of literature or painting. There is a woman present he has a sudden desire to lie with. She may be the wife of some other man in the group. Naturally he says nothing of his sudden desire aloud.

Nevertheless he says it and she answers. She would also rather like it, or she would like it not.

Someone in the group is lying. No one questions aloud what he he is saying, but we do question. "He is lying now," the under voices cry back and forth. Always this under, unspoken communication between people, a constant flow. Often I think no man really ever succeeds in lying to another.

It is possible at times, I think, to get into the flow, the under voices becoming audible. It may even be that this is what the mind, when it is wandering, running, leaping, as described by Verga*, is really seeking, to connect itself with the flow.

No one ha(s) ever been able to entirely control this flow. It is undoubtedly controlled at times, even for long periods, in the consummation of some work of art. When I was at Olivet and had looked at some work turned in by one of the students and it was time for me to talk with the student, I took him or her into my car. I refused to quibble over words and sentences put down. That did not interest me. In all of the stories, novels, etc., I saw there was the same lack of respect for the characters in the imagined world they were trying to create.

People pushed here and there in the imagined world. There was a constant violence being done these people. Some scheme for a story or novel had come into the writer's mind. They were making the characters

*De Vries's letter, to which this is an answer, quotes from *"Cavalleria Rusticana*, by Giovanni Verga" in *Phoenix: The Posthumous Papers of D.H. Lawrence*, edited by Edward D. Macdonald (New York, The Viking Press, 1936.)

of the story or novel do this or that to fit into the scheme thought out. Something false there. Often horrible violence done to these people. As though I, a writer, had a right to do as I pleased with people carried into an imagined life.

The thing never understood was the sacredness of that life too.

The obligation to that life, to my mind, is greater than to the characters in what we call real life. If there is any such thing as real life, reality. I often doubt there is. In real life the character you see can at least fight back. He can deny the lie you tell about him.

Have you not often read a story where a character has been made by the storyteller to do something you knew the character could not do? We call it bad art. It is more than that. It is a display of immorality.

What is needed among so-called artists is moral men who will not do this violence to people in their imagined world. That is what the world is seeking, a morality. To my mind the place to find it is in an attitude first of all, to this imagined life. Sincerely yours

--Letter to Carrow De Vries, August 9, 1939, from *Letters of Sherwood Anderson*, #379

I have been in a state—horrible depression. It comes on sometimes like a disease. What is it? One knows that when work is put out, little spiteful things will be said here and there. One tries to close the ears, go along, but there are always people who write spiteful letters too.

--Letter to Alfred Stieglitz and Georgia O'Keeffe, December 7, 1923, from *Letters of Sherwood Anderson*, # 91

Some few men have done me the honor to say that I have some instinctive knowledge of painting. To tell the truth, I think I have. This man is a painter. I myself have bought three of his things, and if I could afford it, I would buy more at once.

What I want to do is this: I want to sell to a few of my friends five or six of his paintings at three hundred dollars each to give him a year in the country doing nothing and thinking of nothing but painting. He can live on fifteen hundred dollars a year; as he is frugal and careful and so also is his wife.

As I think you know, I could myself, I believe, put this man across to the public now by beginning to write of his work. I do not want to do that yet. I would like it if he could have several years yet of painting in obscurity.* If such a young man should get some fame now, it might set him back for five years. I know something about this, having got some fame myself and knowing something of what it costs. I dare say I would have been a damned sight better writer today if I could have stayed longer in obscurity thinking of nothing but writing.

On the other hand, I do not believe much in the subsidizing of artists. There is a certain fine self-respect left in a man who earns his own way.

--Letter to Mr. Otto Kahn, January, 26, 1929, from *Letters of Sherwood Anderson*, #155

(Otto Kahn, 1867-1934, banker, member of Kuhn, Loeb and Company.)

*Charles Bockler gave his first exhibition in April, 1929, at the Charcoal Club in Baltimore. For this event Anderson wrote a short "Foreword," saying that he admired the painter's work extremely.

Personally and physically I am a very strong man. I know a little of what an artist among us has to face—misunderstanding often enough, most of all the patronage of inferior men.

I couldn't help hope you had money and, by that token, liberty and leisure. Well, you have an understanding wife and your children. That is much. I also have three children, but cannot live where they are. I see them but two or three times a year.

I want so much for you the quiet leisure that would enable you to develop your talent. You aren't going to get it, I'm afraid.

Now I rather think—in America, at least—survival and development is largely a matter of nerve force, of survival. It may always have been so everywhere. God only knows.

At any rate, you do not face what Dreiser did. Now I think it true that no man can do good work among us without its being known. A small body, at least, of intelligent criticism does grow up. One has to remember that Dreiser waited ten years after *Sister Carrie* before he began to get recognition from Hackett, Dell, Mencken, and others.

I have myself a notion that prose writing can't go on just stating. It has to become more sensually aware of life, color, sound, form. There must be flame and play too; the fabric, the feel of surfaces must be consciously sought after.

--Letter to Roger Sergel, December, 1923, from *Letters of Sherwood Anderson*, #90

...I have spoken a good deal here of my fears but I do not believe that my fears were based on lack of faith in my own talent. I was then as I have always been, not a proud but an infinitely vain man. At bottom I was an egotist, As Ben Hecht once said of me, so much the egotist that nothing ever really touched the central core of my egotism.

"Why, I can write as well as any man alive. I have not come to it yet but I will come to it," I was always secretly saying to myself. Among the men I had known who were interested in books and writing, O. Henry had been time and time again pointed out to me as the great American Story Teller. But I did not think he was great. "He has learned too many tricks," I thought. I thought that Mark Twain, in his *Huckleberry Finn*, and Melville, in his *Moby Dick*, had been our great tale tellers. I was myself a man outside the schools. At the time I had not come to Chekhov or to Turgenev in his *Annals of a Sportsman*, but I had found the delightful and swaggering George Borrow. I was, I knew, in a curious position. Although I had been a passionate reader, my reading had never had any fixed direction. There were whole continents of literature that I had never visited. My own vocabulary was small. I had no Latin and no Greek, no French. When I wanted to arrive at anything like delicate shades of meaning in my writing I had to do it with my own very limited vocabulary.

And even my reading had not much increased my vocabulary. Oh, how many words I knew in books that I could not pronounce.

But should I use in my writing words that were not a part of my own everyday speech, of my own everyday thought?

I did not think so.

"No," I had long been telling myself, "you will have to stay where you have put yourself." There was the language of the streets, of American towns and cities, the language of the factories and warehouses where I had worked, of laborers' rooming houses, the saloons, the farms.

"It is my own language, limited as it is. I will have to learn to work with it. There was a kind of poetry I was seeking in my prose, word to be laid against word in just a certain way, a kind of word color, a match of words and sentences, the color to be squeezed out of simple words, simple sentence construction." Just how much of all of this had been thought out, as I have spoken of it here, I do not now know. What I do know is the fact of my awareness of the limitations I had to face; my feeling that the writing, the telling of tales had got too far away from the manner in which we men of the time were living our lives.

--from *Sherwood Anderson's Memoirs*, "Book III, A Robin's Egg Renaissance, 5. Margy Currie"

The impressions gathered by a writer, let us say, in the first twenty years of his life, impressions of people, and events experienced during these formative years when the imagination is most alive, are bound to become source materials for him all his life, and often you have to go far back into childhood to recapture some of these impressions that become materials.

--from *Sherwood Anderson's Memoirs*, "Book 1, What A Man's Made Of, 5. Experiments"

When it comes to our Mr. Ring Lardner, here is something else again. Here is another word fellow, one who cares about the words of our American speech and who is perhaps doing more than any other American to give new force to the words of our everyday life.

There is something I think I understand about Mr. Ring Lardner. The truth is that I believe there is something the matter with him and I have a fancy I know what it is. He is afraid of the highbrows. They scare him to death. I wonder why. For it is true that there is often, in a paragraph of his, more understanding of life, more human sympathy, more salty wisdom than in hundreds of pages of, say Mr. Sinclair Lewis's dreary prose—and I am sure Mr. Lewis would not hesitate to outface any highbrow in his lair.

I said that I thought I knew what was the matter with Mr. Ring Lardner. He comes from out in my country, from just such another town as the one in which I spent my own boyhood, and I remember certain shy lads of my own town who always made it a point to consort mostly with the town toughs—and for a reason. There was in them something extremely sensitive that did not want to be hurt. Even to mention the fact that there was in such a one a real love of life, a quick sharp stinging hunger for beauty would have sent a blush of shame to his cheeks. He was intent upon covering up, concealing from everyone, at any cost, the shy hungry child he was carrying about within himself.

--from *Sherwood Anderson's Notebook*, "Four American Impressions, #2"

It is bad for the writer to associate with the kind of writers we now produce. To associate with their wives is even worse. The men sometimes have moments of being ashamed. The wives never. These men have made a business of writing. They speak and talk of nothing else.

They call it "work." Such conversations as this always go on.

"I am at my desk at night."

"I work until twelve."

"How are things going with you?" says one.

He means, how are your pencils holding up.

The wives chatter endlessly—always about writing.

Such men make money and collect things—old furniture, rare editions. They are like bankers trying to prove their culture. A worried, nervous, useless crew.

I would rather be a Negro deckhand on a steamboat.

Give me for associates, farmers, cattle buyers, railroad men, sailors, small merchants, taxi drivers.

How can a man grow rich writing who has good taste?

Good taste is as necessary to friendship as breath to the body.

When I have been a long time away from the haunts of writers I forget what they are like. I go to New York or Paris. God only knows how gladly I escape these places.

--from *Sherwood Anderson's Memoirs*, "Book VI, Life, Not Death— 4. Writers Sweet and Sour"

...I had been using the words of our human speech, really to deceive men. I was making and selling paint and there was no doubt that houses needed painting; and if all of this reasoning of a quite ordinary man as he walks along the streets of an Ohio town alone, say on a moonlit night, having just come from the shop of his friend (Luther Pawsey—author 's note), an obscure little printer, seems somewhat primitive and simple it at least should be of interest as revealing what must go on in many such men.

The questions asked, defenses made. The real implications of what Luther was at that time saying to me were that I was sinning in some odd way in writing my paint circulars rather well. A great deal of the business that at that time came to me was done by mail, and to create confidence in the breast of some man at a distance, who had never seen you, knew nothing of you personally, it was of course necessary to write well.

It was quite true that in writing anything...for example a paint circular...the object sought was some sort of an entrance into the confidence of the other man and so, even in such a crude approach to the art of writing, you thought, not of the thing about which you were presumed to be talking, but of the man addressed. "Now how can I win his confidence?" you thought and this led inevitably to the secret of watching men.

So you went about in life, always a bit on the alert, listening, watching. In modern society you were like a little animal in a jungle. It was a question of survival. Some men were strong. They fought and bullied others.

Others were shrewd and sharp. They could think faster than other men, take advantage quicker.

And you?

Perhaps you had none of these qualities so you developed another. You had found out that words could throw men off their guard and so you began, more and more, to use words to serve your own private ends...

...and all the time also using them to keep up the illusion in others that you were really naïve, quite innocent, had nothing but their good, rather than your own good in mind...

...this never however done too obviously. You watched yourself always to grow more and more skillful.

It is to be borne in mind that I had been at this thing...this advertising writing, for several years. An accident had led me into being an advertising man.

But was it an accident?

...you must think of me now as going along a street in an Ohio town and arguing with myself, much as I am doing here...

Walking at night through the night streets of an Ohio town, after one of my talks with Luther, he having put his finger on something in me...love of words... "you have a kind of talent in the use of simple words..." "occasionally, when you try, you can make a sentence..." "it's rather a shame, really, Sherwood, for you to be in the bunko game you are in."

These little knives stuck into me by Luther, left sticking in me. I walked uncomfortably, coming from his shop. Sometimes, even though it was raining and my clothes were wet, I didn't go home. I think I must have been made over and over to myself the kind of protest most men make.

I think it not unlikely that I had been able to go into my house and sit down, call my wife and children to me, and say to them... "here, you. Listen to me. I am a man born with a certain sort of talent and I have just discovered it in myself. I have been dreaming a dream, a childish sort of dream but I am beginning to awaken. As for you, my wife and children, if you have got off on the wrong track in life, it is not your fault, but now we must right about face..." had I been able to explain to them all might have been well.

I felt myself unable to explain. Oh land of the free, what is freedom? I think that my notion of the life of the writer, a possibility a little opened up to me by Luther's words... "I might be able to do it," I found myself saying to myself...afterwards when I did become a writer and began telling tales it was said of me by critics that all of my tales were of one sort...they were stories of escape...it must have seemed to me then, as for that matter it does yet, that the real tale of American lives is as yet just that.

...eternal fleeing from something.

... "I will." "I won't." "I will." "I won't."...

... "it is the fault of this woman. I will flee from her"...

... "I can do nothing in this town"...

... "city life may save me"...

... "no. It is not that. I will flee from the city to the town, from the town to the country..."

It must have been that upon me, as upon all men, rested a responsibility. How loath we are to take it. Upon me, an obscure and scheming little paint maker, dreaming my dream of riches to be acquired, great houses to be lived in, myself clambering up to all of this over the shoulders of others, dragging after me my wife and children, a penny lifted out of the pocket of this man, a dime out of the pocket of that man, slow accumulation at first, then faster. Now you have more elbow room. Now you may begin to play with thousands, not hundreds.

Really big men playing with railroads, whole railroad systems, chains of newspapers, great oil companies, chains of retail stores...

...bigger and bigger you grow. Now there are gigantic children playing with gigantic toys and you are one of them...

All this, as I have suggested, after starting home from Luther's shop....How much of the starting of this in me he intended I'll never know,--but having, as suggested, started homeward, I did not go home. And wandering in the streets at night, schemes began coming into my head. It was at this time, and under the influence of Luther, who never spoke of politics, that I became a socialist.

--from *Sherwood Anderson's Memoirs*, "Book II, American Money, 8. The Man of Ideas"

...We live in a world in which most of the channels of public expression are ruled by the advertisers, and it is difficult to write of human life, giving yourself to the life immediately about you, without getting upon forbidden ground.

It can be done. Trick writing can be learned. It is a trade, not an art. It may be all right. Formerly I used to grow indignant because so many writers seemed to be selling out. Now I think it doesn't matter. I think every man writes as well as he can. Ordinary people need to be amused, taken away from thought. Life itself is too terribly real for them. We hear of great statesmen, scientists, etc., who spend their leisure hours reading detective stories. Why not? The statesman might begin thinking of how he got to where he is. The scientists had made some great discovery, but he is using his knowledge for his own private ends. He is no better or worse than the rest of us. But above all things he doesn't want to think.

We live, you see, in a thin age. We can't take it. There may have been times, periods in the history of man, when man did face the moral obligation of living. In our age we can't do it. Don't blame us too much.

I have become a veteran among American writers. Where have the years gone? How little I have done.

Young writers, new men among writers, are always writing letters to me. They come to see me. "How can I write as I please and still make a living?" It is a question for which I have no answer. To tell the truth, I am not interested in how you make a living.

I am interested only in what you give me, in how much you extend my own knowledge of life. You came from a different environment. You were born in a rich or a well-to-do family, while I came from a poor one.

What was the tone of life in your house? How did you feel? What made you what you are?

There are a thousand questions I want to ask you. Tell me in your work. Tell me. Tell me. The tales you tell, the way you tell them, the tone, color, form, all of these should reveal yourself to me. Give me a little of yourself. Extend a little my own knowledge, my own capacity for feeling, for understanding. I am a lustful man. I want everything. I knew a painter once who said to me, "I want to make love to a thousand, a hundred thousand women." I understand him. He didn't really want to bed the women. He wanted to go into them, penetrate into the mystery of women. It was because of something he wanted in his art.

It seems to me that we shall have more and more writing. People, it seems to me, are becoming more conscious of thinness. Now (a)days I myself no longer hope or want to be a popular writer. I write for myself and for other writers. It doesn't matter to me now that I am often misunderstood. I have come to realize that I have dreadful limitations. Once I thought, I will write so well, so clearly, will tell my tales so clearly, with such verve and gusto that everyone must accept me, but now I do not care for such acceptance. If you are mine, I cannot lose you. If I am yours, I will remain yours.

It is a way of making love. It is a way of losing self. It must be that the painter, as he paints, becomes always more and more conscious of nature, its moods, of the strange beauty coming unexpectedly out of what seem to others commonplace scenes. Why should I care whether you, the young writer, have had your breakfast, whether or not you have money to pay your rent or buy a car? I care only that you may broaden my own vision, increase my own capacity to feel, add a little to my understanding of others.

--Letter to George Freitag, August 27, 1938, from *Letters of Sherwood Anderson*, #343

...I was finishing another novel called *Dark Laughter*. How easy to say "finishing." But oh, the pain of doing it.

You have the idea and you begin; but what hours and often days between the beginning of your book and its end...if you ever get to the end. How easy to have it slip away from you.

There are these characters, with which you start. Others come in. There is a character you thought to have play a minor role but suddenly he or she is all over your book.

And you have your theme, to which you are trying to hold. There is the necessity of a movement forward, something growing as a child grows in a pregnant woman. The whole also to be orchestrated, innumerable false starts abandoned, pages and pages, sometimes thousands of words, put down that must be thrown aside.

And then, later, something else. You have your book, your novel, at last in manuscript, and then it must go into type.

Why, here is something else again. Now, in this form, you stand a little away from it. Its intimacy with you is gone. The book is one thing in manuscript and another in type. There is this dread of seeing it thus, the trembling fear, the hope.

"Will it stand up to this?"

For hours you have been sitting at your desk, the words flowing out from under your fingers. There is something you have long been trying to get that you think you have at last got.

And then the reaction comes. There has been this intense concentration and now you are striving to come out of it. You go to walk. Sometimes I have found that drink helps at such times. You have been in one world and you are trying to return to another. Your nerves are jumpy.

And so, on this day of early spring, I was in this condition and walked in the street. I saw people, houses, cars, passing in the street without seeing. I had gone through several streets and had got down to the water front and while thus walking, half blind, trying to shake off the intense mood that had gripped me I was approached by a sailor.

He had apparently been on a long drunk. His voice was husky. He had in his mouth an unlighted cigarette. He approached me noiselessly and with a kind of supreme effort shouted in my ear.

"Hey, boss, give me a match," he said and I jumped.

It was as though someone had shot off a gun in my face. I was very angry. I turned on him. I began to curse. It is a wonder he did not knock me down.

"You damn fool," I shouted, "to so approach a man, startle him." I stood there cursing, calling him all the ugly names I could think of but he only laughed at me. Stepping a little away he eyed me with shrewd bleary eyes.

"Oh," he said, "I see, I see, a nervous proposition." It seemed to explain everything and he went away laughing and as he went he kept looking back at me.

"Oho! Oho! I see! I see! A nervous proposition," he kept repeating as he went.

Nervous or not, I wandered on. I was again nearly broke. Within a few days, I thought I would be compelled to go back again to Chicago and to the writing of advertisements...I was walking thus when unexpectedly I ran into a man who was to become a real influence in my life and in my affairs.

It was that strange character, much maligned, much misunderstood, the strangest man, I am sure, ever in the publishing business in America. I am speaking of Horace Liveright.

He was then and, for that matter, until the end of his life, a very handsome man, tall and erect, his hair just touched with gray. He walked with an easy swing and when I saw him that day in New Orleans, he was accompanied by a very beautiful woman.

There was an absurd mistake made. Already I knew Horace Liveright, had been with him on several occasions in New York. He was the publisher of my friend, Theodore Dreiser, and of another friend, Eugene O'Neill. He was with a beautiful woman and I had seen him with many beautiful women.

"Meet my wife," he said and, "Oh, yeah?" I answered.

There was an uncomfortable moment. It *was* Mrs. Liveright. I was sunk and so was Horace.

"It may have been an uncomfortable moment for you but it was a lot more than that for me," Horace later told me.

However he forgave me. He came to see me later in the same afternoon and we went to drink together and, when he inquired, I told him that I was looking for a new publisher.

"It isn't that I'm not fond of Ben," I said.

"Yes, I understand. We are all fond of Ben," he said.

He made me a proposal that took my breath away. I had spoken to him of the advertising agency. "I'll have to go back there, begin again to write of tooth paste, of kidney pills, of how to keep your hair from falling out." There must have been a note of desperation in my voice and Horace, on that occasion as always with me, was very gentle. We were at a table in the little New Orleans cafe and were drinking. He reached across the table and put his hand on my hand.

"So you are discouraged, eh? You think your books cannot be sold. What nonsense. You come with me." He made a proposal.

"For five years I'll send you a hundred dollars a week. I'll take what you write. I'll sell your books."

--from *Sherwood Anderson's Memoirs*, "Book IV, The Literary Life, 10. Meeting Horace Liveright"

Chapter Three

The Financial Struggle

Will payment equal the quality of our work? Will
we be able to make our living as writers?

Dear Cullen*: I think your letter one of the most generous and friendly I ever got. It touched me where I live. And I don't intend to pinch or cramp your generosity.

First of all, I think I should tell you, quite frankly, about my finances. For a good many years, excepting only one year—and this would cover my whole career as a writer—I have made practically no money.

I did have one year where I made a good deal, largely, I think, because that year I was with a publisher who plunged on advertising. He went broke later...

I had that one fat year and with the money raked in bought me the little farm, here in the Virginia hills, and built the stone house in which I live. You must come down and see me here next summer. I don't stay here in the winter, largely because of the damn sinus that sends me off to seek warmth. The book that paid the bill was the one you like, *Dark Laughter*. I have written others that go deeper and will, in the end, stand up better, but that is another matter.

I was born, Cullen, in 1876, so you can figure how aged I am. On the whole I'm pretty well, except for getting floored about twice a year, but I presume the damn thing does cut down my vitality and my ability to turn out work. It had me in the hospital last winter.

I presume I don't make more money because I don't write the sort of glamorous stuff the popular magazines want, and there have been years, and this since I have been recognized as, well, you know, among American writers, when I haven't made, aside from lecturing, which I detest, two thousand dollars.

So it is a constant struggle, and...

--Letter to John Paul Cullen, September 16, 1937, from *Letters of Sherwood Anderson*, #323

*John Paul Cullen of the Veterans Administration had suggested Anderson's eligibility for a pension as a Spanish-American War veteran.

Such a strange place to be in. I am in a huge western State university. It is night. I have been lecturing on Modern American Writing before a thousand young men and women. What an absurd thing to try to do. There I have been standing, before all these young men and women, talking and talking. How silly! I did it for money. I have been broke and have been lecturing to get some money into my pockets. I would like so well the things money buys—cigarettes, horses, warm clothes, a fine house to live in. I would so like to have a great deal of money. Why does not someone who has ten or fifteen million dollars give me a million, or a half million, anyway? If you meet a man bothered by his money tell him about me. I would like to wear clothes made of delicate fabrics, gay, brightly-colored neckties, flashing vests, plaid socks. I would like a string of race horses, a farm, a yacht. There is in me something that likes to strut before men, make a splash of color in the street where I walk. I do not want the women to wear all of the bright gay things. The little city girl, who works in a factory or in an office and spends all of her money to buy clothing she can ill afford, has won my heart. She is my sister. Long ago, in some old European corner, she and I belonged to the same tribe.

And so I am lecturing to get money to buy the necessities of life and a few gay things, not necessary, for myself, for my wife, for my sons.

But what an odd experience, this lecturing. There are a thousand young men and women in the hall where I have been speaking. What do they think of me, standing up there and trying to say bright wise things to them? As I talked I had an idea. I shall propose it to my lecture manager. It is inconceivable to me that anyone should want to come to hear any man lecture. Perhaps students are bullied into it. Husbands are brought by wives who are after culture and who have the erroneous notion that I am cultured. I shall propose to my manager a scheme. People may hear me lecture for 25 cents but shall be charged $1 for the privilege of staying away. Millions will want to stay away. We shall both grow rich like a prize fighter and his manager. I have such brilliant business ideas.

The lecturing excites me. When I come out on the platform something happens. There is an actor sleeping in me and now he is awake. I stand, pause for effect, I become for the moment something I have never been before, walk in a new way, look at people out of new eyes. The world of the actor opens before me. What a strange world it is. Now this being, that is myself, is longer myself. My body, my voice, my mind are instruments I have to learn to play. I do it badly enough.

I have lectured in the large hall and most of the people who have heard me have gone away. There are, however, twenty or thirty young men and women who have got me into a smaller room and are asking me questions.

Lord God of the mountains and valleys preserve me! Every question is so fundamental. These people now firing questions at me want to become writers in their turn. They are asking me how to do it and I am trying to answer. My bitterest enemy would be glad if he could see me now, if he knew how silly and helpless I feel inside myself. Had I never any modesty? What has become of it? I am actually trying to answer the questions. I think of Ben and Paul and Joe—wits all of them. In fancy I can see Ben giving an imitation of me as a lecturer. Thank Heavens, they are not here!

Why is money so hard to come by? There is so much of it about. If you see the man with the superfluous million do remember my name. It may be he is worried about his income tax. Tell him I shall not worry.

--from *Sherwood Anderson's Notebook*, "When The Writer Talks"*

*Published in *The Literary Review*, 1925

Dear Brother Burrow: Have you read my new book, *Winesburg?* The book has been getting rather remarkable recognition even from those who have fought me before. In another year it will no doubt get publication in France and perhaps in other European countries.

Naturally I am very anxious to continue my work as a writer, but the truth is that I am rapidly approaching the time when I shall have to give it up. It begins to look as though, having made myself this tool of expression by infinite labor, I shall have to put it aside.

The situation with me is one that you will readily understand. For twenty years I have carried a double load, making my living as a writer of advertisements and trying always to steal as much time as possible for this other work. Unfortunately I have not made much money, a living only as I have gone along. Now I begin to tire. For weeks and months at a time now I find that the reserve of energy I have always had is gone. The long hours of work in an office every day begins to take the strength I need for my writing.

As you no doubt know, there is no money to be got by writing the sort of books I write. A copy of such a book is read by ten people to every one who purchases it. The result is that the author gets little.

In facing what I face now—that is to say, the possibility that I will have to give up the fight—my mind gropes about trying to see some way out. Surely I am willing to live in the very simplest way to accomplish what I want, but I do need some assured income every year. I have three children who have to be supported. In all I need from twenty-five hundred to three thousand a year to live.

Do you think there is any chance at all of my interesting some man or woman of money to back me in this extent in trying to do my work? I know nothing of such things, but do know that money is constantly being invested in schools, magazines, young singers, in a thousand things of the sort.

It seems to me that I have proven my ability as a writer. I know of no other man in this country who has got such recognition as has come to me. Yet I make no money, and it is evident that the only source of income I might expect to open to me, the magazine field, will not open. The editors of such magazines write me personal letters congratulating me on the fine work I am doing, but laugh at the idea of printing my stuff. It is all very perplexing and disconcerting.

It may be possible that the idea of striving to interest some man or woman with money is equally futile. It is a difficult matter to approach. I surely do not know how to do it. Do you think there is a possibility in that direction?

What I want you will understand. The development of my mind and my skill as a workman has brought me to the place where I naturally want to do more and more delicate and subtle work. I want time to go about among people. I want something of leisure to develop in leisure my impression of life. Having made myself an artist by infinite labor, I want to lead the life and do the work of an artist and not have to spend my days writing stupid advertisements.

Surely I have that right. Surely I am not to (o) self-pushing in setting up the claim I do here. Is there any hope at all that someone might be found who would sympathize with my desires enough to help me achieve them?

To tell you the truth, I know of no reason why anyone should do this; that is to say, I know of no reason from their point of view. I may be after all but a man grasping at straws. What do you think about it? Very truly yours

(P.S.) I have lost your Baltimore address.

--Letter to Trigant Burrow, September 15, 1919, from *Letters of Sherwood Anderson*, #41

I have been thinking over this matter, and I believe that when you and your associates also think it over, you will be willing to extend this concession, that is, your taking twenty-five per cent rather than fifty per cent, to cover all reprints.

In your letter you speak of the gamble taken by Mr. Huebsch in becoming my publisher, but, really, I do not think there was such a great gamble. Mr. Huebsch was not my first publisher. The first book he published was my *Winesburg, Ohio,* but already, at that time, I had published two novels and a book of verse, and one of these books had had a marked success for a new writer, selling somewhere between ten and fifteen thousand copies.

It is, of course, quite true that when my *Winesburg, Ohio* was published, it was generally looked upon as being somewhat revolutionary in form. The accepted form of the short story in America had been set by Mr. O. Henry. It is true that I had had some difficulty in getting the book published, but I am sure that Mr. Huebsch never spent much money in publishing it.

I say all of this without intending to reflect in any way upon Mr. Huebsch, a man I look upon as a friend and for whom I have an affectionate regard. It may very well be that, at that time, Mr. Huebsch was in no shape to push my work. He and I have often spoke of this, and I think there is a mutual understanding of what the situation was.

The fact, however, remains that I was, all through the years when Mr. Huebsch was my publisher, always in a rather desperate financial situation. Later, and after I went to another publisher, who was able to spend money pushing my books, I did do better. As I have more than once told Mr. Huebsch, had I known of the prospective reorganization of Mr. Huebsch's publishing business, I never would have left him.

The fact remains that my other publishers, who have handled my books since, that is to say, Liveright and Scribner, have asked and have taken nothing for my foreign rights or my reprints. Some time ago you made a concession in the matter of foreign rights, cutting your share of those rights to twenty-five per cent. You have graciously done the same thing in the particular instance about which we are now having this correspondence. Cannot you now go further and make this concession cover all reprints of my work? I do not think that I am being overly greedy or unfair in asking this. I am no longer a young man and have a family. What rights I have in my lifetime of literary efforts is about all I have to leave to my wife and family. I do think and believe you will agree with me, that in this matter there is something more involved than an ordinary business matter.

--Letter to Mr. Marshall A. Best, The Viking Press, Inc., New York, June 21, 1937, from *Letters of Sherwood Anderson*, #318

You see my position, Ben. You must know, having been my publisher, what a rather tough struggle for existence I have had. For years, while I was writing these stories, some of which are from time to time reprinted, I had to go on being an advertising writer, an occupation I detested. You know what a tough struggle for existence I have had. As a writer I have chosen always what has seemed to me the artist's way. We will say nothing of what ability I may have developed, but this I think I can say—that I have never gone cheap on the art of writing, in the sense of doing cheap or flashy writing. I have at least clung to a certain sincerity of purpose.

And now, after all these years, I do, now and then, have a chance to get in a little much-needed money. Here is a story, out of a book you published years ago and that perhaps not now even is kept in print. This magazine, *Redbook,* is, it seems, willing to pay five hundred dollars to reproduce the story. The check is sent to you, and you keep and use the money for several months. The agent takes his ten per cent, and out of the five hundred dollars I finally get, after several months of waiting, two hundred, twenty-five dollars.

Do you really think this is fair, Ben? I am not a businessman. I am an artist struggling to live and do my work. I think I may fairly say I have had some influence on writing in America. I may perhaps even have influenced other writers whose books your house now publishes. At least these writers have written me and said so. My struggle has been a long, hard one. I know that technically, and legally, you probably have a right to half (of) any monies paid to me for the reprinting of old stories, some of them only written after years of effort, but do you not really believe, Ben, that in these cases, that is to say, the reprinting of my old stories, it would be fairer for your firm to be satisfied with twenty-five per cent and that I might have the needed money without several months of waiting?

I put this matter up to you and your fellows in your firm. I do think, Ben, that mine is somewhat a special case. I am very grateful for the permission you recently gave me to use materials from my *Winesburg* stories in my book of plays and for the concession you made me some years ago in reducing your share on translations of my works, controlled by you, from fifty per cent to twenty-five per cent, but I do think that, as I have a sore need of any monies my work may earn, that now, after all these years, this other concession might well be made to me.

I write all of this to you, Ben, without bitterness, but certainly with a good deal of hope that you and your fellows there may accept my point of view. Sincerely

--Letter to Mr. Ben Huebsch, June 12, 1937, from *Letters of Sherwood Anderson*, #316

...While I suppose my position in letters is pretty well established in America, I have never made much of any money. It has been hard sledding all along, and I have not wanted to go in for the popular magazines or the movies. On the other hand, I do not want any money at all if my own work can provide me a living, but I believe if I could have a guarantee of say $3,000.00 a year for the next three or four years, we could get some of this material into the theatre in a very effective way. I would like to make my farm down in Virginia a center for work with other men during the summers and do the traveling in the winter. If any of my books or plays begin to sell in a way that makes an allowance from the fund unnecessary, it should be stopped.

This, my dear Adelaide, is about as close as I can get in a letter to my situation, my plans, and my dreams. I am tremendously grateful to you and am grateful to Mr. Moe for his interest. If nothing can be done, I will not stop being grateful. Sincerely

--Letter to Adelaide Walker*, before March 22nd., 1933, from *Letters of Sherwood Anderson*, # 230

*Adelaide George Walker and her husband, Charles Rumford Walker, were at this time preparing to establish a workers' theater, later the Theater Union, and had suggested that Anderson apply to the Guggenheim Foundation for financial assistance in order to write labor plays.

A few months earlier he had come to me. He had wanted very much to buy the manuscript of my *Winesburg*.

"Did it exist?"

"Yes. It existed."

The book had been written on pages of a cheap tablet. The manuscript existed only because a certain woman, at the moment in love with me, had collected the scrawled sheets, thrown carelessly aside and had saved them.

So the manuscript had been saved, and later, when it began to have some value, I had managed—because the woman who had saved it had died—by lying to her sister, by telling the sister that the dead woman had only been keeping it for me, by such slickness I had got it back.

So there it was in my possession, and did I value it?

I did not.

I had been told that, some day, it would bring money.

Well, I wanted money. I was no fool. Well enough I knew that without money the artist man is helpless.

So there had been this rich man who had come to me wanting to buy this manuscript, and I had been shrewd.

Was I shrewd or had a moment of honesty come to me?

I had not yet sold the rich man the manuscript.

I had laughed at the man.

"But why do you want them, these sheets of cheap paper upon which certain tales have been scrawled?"

I had told the rich man that his wanting the sheets upon which certain stories had been scribbled was like wanting an old dress discarded by a woman rather than the woman herself.

--from *Sherwood Anderson's Memoirs*, "Book IV, The Literary Life, 5. Certain Meetings South"

...I have been thinking for several years that we would presently grow tired of the rather hard-boiled, pessimistic, wisecracking attitude toward life. In fact I have sometimes said to myself that we are again in a dark age that clings to the belief that a good life may be attained through economic readjustment alone. It is pretty hopeless.

I do suppose that such a magazine as you have in mind would have to be subsidized, and here there comes in something that has often been in my mind about the subsidized magazines. I think it was so of the old *Seven Arts*, of the short-lived *Freeman's Magazine*, and I believe it to be true of the *New Republic*. I don't know exactly why it is true, but so many of our writers are terribly up against the problem of making a living. Often these subsidized magazines have seemed to use up most of the subsidy in paying a staff of editors. The writers have been asked to send in what is sometimes their finest work and are paid little or nothing, while often the editors are rather well paid.

Of course, I know this is an old, old problem. The number of people who subsist between the artists and the publisher is always rather tremendous. I do think that if anything can be done to correct this a little, it should be done.

--Letter to Miss Dorothy Norman*, June 14, 1937, from *Letters of Sherwood Anderson*, # 317

*In 1938 Dorothy Norman began editing *Twice a Year*, a "journal of the arts, and civil liberties." This is the proposed magazine which is being discussed in the letter.

...To get the stories (i.e., *Winesburg*—author's note) published was a harder matter. In New York *The Seven Arts* and the old *Masses*, in Chicago *The Little Review* had begun printing them and in one or two instances I got as much as ten dollars for one of them. Once later I counted up—it must have been in a base moment, when I was thinking of money. For the whole series, printed in this way, I figured I had got eighty-five dollars. I mention the matter because I am always getting letters from young writers and they seem, most of them, to be up against what I was up against.

They want freedom to write. "How am I to make a living?" they ask, but unfortunately while our manufacturers, as for example our automobile manufacturers, seem to have been able to make the public pay for their experiments, we who experiment in prose and in verse cannot do it.

Often the new writer, addressing me thus, seems to feel that I, being somewhat established, have got hold of some secret. There is, they seem to think, a key, a golden key that one finds and with which one at once begins to open doors. They want to borrow the key. They have read, perhaps, romantic stories of writers. There is a man of rare but unrecognized talent who has been living in a garret. He is down to his last crust of bread. He eats the crust and, with the strength thus got, writes a story or poem. He sends it off to a publisher but as he has been unable to pay his rent he is kicked out of his room.

So there he is. It is a dark rainy night and he spends it on a park bench and, in the morning he awakens, very hungry and also stiff and sore, but, at that moment, blown by the wind, a part of one of the city's morning newspapers...it would be the front page...lands at his feet. He looks down and there is his name, in big type, staring at him. He has got fame. A new genius is born and some editor, or publisher, filled with excitement, has been announcing him to the world.

The above, to be sure, exaggerated, but having in it the nub of the matter. There is something that the young writer believes if I but would, I could do; some secret I could let him in on.

--from *Sherwood Anderson's Memoirs*, "Book IV, The Literary Life, 1. Waiting for Ben Huebsch"

...I am very grateful for these early years of poverty. So many men I have known have been so frightened all their lives by fear of poverty in old age. It is what has kept their noses to the grindstone while I have often walked free. It is true that I remember whole winters when there was no such thing as white flour in our house. There was, during a whole winter, no butter to spread on bread. Well, what of it? We got a little corn meal. More eating of corn bread would I'm sure make a better foundation for an American literature. The white bread we eat is to corn bread what Hollywood will be to real American dramatic literature when it comes...

--from *Sherwood Anderson's Memoirs*, "Book I, What A Man's Made Of, 7. New Worlds"

...*Many Marriages* sold well, and I have assurance of a year's living ahead. No artist dare ask more. I let the bourgeois worry about right and wrong, morals, respectability, and money in the bank. My plan shouldn't work, but it does, so I ride along. I believe a bookseller at Boston got arrested and fined $200 for selling my last book in Boston, where it was outlawed by some local purity law, but then he no doubt was getting $5 or $10 a copy. The distiller must make his beverage, I presume, and not worry about an occasional bootlegger...

--Letter to Karl Anderson, May 31, 1923, from *Letters of Sherwood Anderson*, #78

Dear Church: I have been intending to write to you for a long time. There has been nothing to say. You were at work. I have worked but little, and what I have done has not been very satisfactory to me. How absurd that you should always hear from me when I am in such a dissatisfied state. It is better not to write.

However, now I am in somewhat of a better temper, having come to a resolution. I have decided that, for my soul's good, I have got to give up the notion of living by writing. The idea that one must produce constantly, or starve, is terribly detrimental to any sort of freedom of approach.

All the time I am driven by this demon of necessity. I am a great fool, Church. When I have made some money, I spend it as though it would last forever. For example, my coming to Europe last year was a great folly. I am constantly spending what I have not got to spend.

I have decided that for my own good I have got to begin making my living. An opportunity has apparently offered (itself.) In a neighboring town, Marion, Virginia, a town of about four thousand people, there is a small weekly newspaper. I have an opportunity to buy it. It is earning about six thousand a year.

You know what such papers are. They are filled with local news, deaths, the small affairs of a prosperous small town, half industrial, half a marketing town for a rather rich agricultural section. Even as I write you, I am planning to go to New York to see if I can raise five thousand dollars, the amount necessary to buy the paper. The money and what else I pay for it on notes I shall expect to get back from the paper itself. It is already prosperous and well established. There is a good local printing business and no competition.

I am taking this step for two reasons: first, to free myself from the immediate necessity of living by my pen, and then to get back into closer association with all kinds of people in their everyday lives. I want to free myself from the necessity of professionalism.

Of course it may not work; that is to say, I may not be able to raise the money. In that case I shall probably go back to some city and get a job.

I guess you know that when we were in California, I made an arrangement with Boni and Liveright by which they were to guarantee me a certain amount for a certain number of years. I was afraid of the proposal, but was driven into it by necessity. They have been very nice, but the situation has always been on my nerves. I cannot get over the idea of being at work for them as an employee. When a day or week comes that I do not write satisfactorily, I am beside myself.

Well, you see, I want what writing I do to be incidental, a part of my life, not a profession. I am seeking a profession outside that.

Over here the *Testament** has brought down a furor on my head. It is much the same sort of thing that greeted *Many Marriages*. My death as a writer is being tolled up and down the literary press. The crapehangers have all been busy. Well, I have been thrown that before. It does not matter much.

However, the other thing does matter. I must earn my living outside my writing, learn to wait. I cannot possibly do a good book a year. It may be that what I shall want to write in the future will sell less readily than in the past.

In the meantime I am having apparently a fine German success...

--Letter to Ralph Church, September 28, 1927, from *Letters of Sherwood Anderson*, #146

**A New Testament* (1927).

Chapter Four

Frustration

What road blocks can be expected in this occupation?

...When a new book or story of mine is printed I read it once, shuddering to think how much I have missed of what I was trying for, and never read it again.

--from *Sherwood Anderson's Memoirs*, "Book I, What A Man's Made Of, 5. Experiments"

...I think that at this period I had an illusion regarding publishers. It was to the effect that they might be interested in writing...

--from *Sherwood Anderson's Memoirs*, "Book IV, The Literary Life, 1. Waiting for Ben Huebsch"

...what the *Dial* is up to I can't quite make out. They give me their prize and buy my novel and publish it, and then seem to devote themselves to a kind of apology to the public for me.

--Letter to Van Wyck Brooks, early October, 1923, # 87, from *Letters of Sherwood Anderson,* #87

A magazine having a circulation of a million is in a rather ticklish position when it comes to handling any such matter as honest reactions to life. There are so many things the editors of all such magazines have to be careful about. All such basic human attributes as sex hungers, greed and the sometimes twisted and strangely perverted desires for beauty in human beings have to be let alone. The basic stuff of human life that all real artists, working in the medium of prose, have handled all through the history of writing has to be thrown aside. The writer is perpetually called upon to seem to be doing something while doing nothing at all. There is the perpetual tragedy of unfulfillment.

Every intelligent man knows that, since Eve tempted Adam with the apple, no such thing as a pure man or woman has ever existed in the world but these poor devils are compelled to believe, against all the dictates of their common sense, that purity is a kind of universal human attribute and departure from it a freakish performance. In order that none of the million subscribers be lost or any good advertiser offended they are forced to spend their lives firing off blank cartridges or shooting pith-balls at pig bladder.

--from *Sherwood Anderson's Notebook*, "Notes on Standardization"

"Can't you, sir, sell one of the stories to some magazine? I am needing money."

He answered my letter. He is a sensible man, knows his business.

"I admit that the stories you have sent me are good stories. But," he said, "you are always getting something into all of your stories that spoils the sale."

He did not go further but I know what he meant.

"Look here," he once said to me, "why don't you, for the time at least, drop this rather intimate style of yours?"

He smiled when he said it and I also smiled.

"Let us say, now, that you are yourself the editor of one of our big American magazines. You have yourself been in business. When you first began to write, even after you had published some of your earlier books, you had to go on for years, working in an advertising place. You must know that all of our large American magazines are business ventures. It costs a great deal of money to print and distribute hundreds of thousands of copies. Often, as you know, the price received for the magazine, when sold on the newsstand, does not pay for the paper on which it is printed."

"Yes, I know."

"They have to have stories that please people."

"Yes, I know."

We had stopped to have a drink at a bar. But a few weeks before he had written me a letter. "There is a certain large magazine that would like to have a story from you. It should be, let us say, a story of about ten thousand words. Do not attempt to write the story. Make an outline, I should say a three- or four-page outline. I can sell the story for you."

I made the outline and sent it to him. "It is splendid," he wrote. "Now you can go ahead. I can get such and such a sum."

"Oh!" The sum mentioned would get me out of my difficulties.

"I will get busy," I said to myself. "In a week I will dash off the story."

Some two or three weeks before, a man friend had come to me one evening. He is a man to whom I am deeply attached.

"Come and walk with me," he said, and we set out afoot, leaving the town where he lived. I had gone to the town to see him but, when I got to his town, there was a sudden illness in his house. The man has children and two of them were in bed with a contagious disease.

I stayed at a hotel. He came there. We walked beyond the town, got into a dirt road, passed farmhouses, dogs barked at us. We got into a moonlit meadow.

We had walked for a long time in silence. At the hotel I had noticed that my friend was in a tense, excited mood.

"You are in some sort of trouble. Is it the children? Has the disease taken a turn for the worse?"

"No," he said. "The children are better. They are all right."

We were in the moonlit meadow, standing by a fence, some sheep grazing nearby and it was a delicious night of the early summer.

"There is something I have to tell to someone," he said. "I wrote to you, begged you to come here."

My friend is a highly respected man in the town.

He began talking. He talked for hours. He told me a story of a secret life he had been living.

My friend is a man of fifty. He is employed as an experimental scientist by a large manufacturing company.

But I might as well confess at once that I am, as you the reader may have guessed, covering the trail of my friend. I am a man rather fortunate in life. I have a good many men friends. If I make this one an experimental scientist working for a large manufacturing company, it will do.

His story was, on the whole, strange. It was like so many stories, not invented but coming directly out of life. It was a story having in it certain so-called sordid touches, strange impulses come to a man of fifty in the grip of an odd passion.

"I have been doing this.

"I have been doing that.

"I have to unload, to tell someone.

"I have been suffering."

My friend did unload his story, getting a certain relief talking to me of a turn in his life that threatened to destroy the position he had achieved in his community. He had got a sudden passion for a woman of his town, the sort of thing always happening in towns. "Three years ago," he said to me, "there was another man here, a friend, a man, as I am, of standing in our community, who did what I am doing now. He became enamored of a woman here, the wife of a friend, and began to meet her secretly.

"At least he thought, or hoped, he was meeting her secretly.

"He did as I have been doing. In the evening when darkness came, he got into his car. She had walked out along a street and in some dark place along the street he picked her up. He drove with her out along little side roads, went to distant towns but soon everyone knew.

"And how I blamed him. I went to him. 'What a fool you are being,' I said to him.

" 'Yes, but I cannot help it. This is the great love of my life.'

" 'What nonsense,' I said. I pled with him, quarreled with him, but it did no good. I thought him an utter fool and now I am being just such another."

I had taken the man with whom I talked in the field, and his story, as the basis for the story I was to write for one of the popular magazines, had made an outline that was pronounced splendid by my agent.

But what rough places I had smoothed out.

"No, I cannot say that such a figure holding such a respectable place in my life did that. There must not be anything unpleasant. There must be nothing that will remind readers of certain sordid moments, thoughts, passions, acts, in their own lives if I am to get this money—and, oh, how I need it."

I am no Shakespeare, but did not even Shakespeare write a play he called *As You Like It?*

"When you are writing to please people you must not touch certain secret, often dark little recesses, that are in all humans.

"Keep in the clear, man. Go gaily along.

"It will be all right to startle them a little.

"You must get a certain dramatic force into your story."

But that night the man, upon whose story I have based the story I am about to write, was, as he talked, simply broken. He even put his face down upon the top rail of the fence, there in that moonlit meadow, and cried. I went to him. I put my arms about his shoulders, said words to him.

"This passion that has come to you at this time in your life, that now threatens to tear down all you have so carefully built up, that threatens to destroy the lives of others you love, will pass.

"At our age, everything passes."

I do not remember just what I did say to him.

And so I began to write, but alas...

Our difficulty is that as we write we become interested, absorbed, often a little in love with these characters of our stories that seem to be growing here, under our hand.

I have begun this story, taking off, as it were, from the story told me in the meadow by my friend; but now, as I write, he has disappeared.

There is a new man, coming to life, here. He seems to be here in this room where I work.

"You must do me right now," he seems to be saying to me.

"There is a certain morality involved," he says.

"Now you must tell everything, put it all down. Do not hesitate. I want it all put down."

At this point there was a series of letters concerning a story to be written that lay on my desk. I had had them brought to me from my files.

"If you are to write the story for us it would be well for you to keep certain things in mind.

"The story should be concerned with the lives of people who are in what might be called comfortable circumstances.

"Above all, it should not be too gloomy.

"We want you to understand that we do not wish, in any way, to dictate to you."

I had sat down to write the tale, for which I had made an outline, in bitter need of the money it might bring. After twenty-five years of writing, some twenty to twenty-five books published, my name up as one of the outstanding American writers of my day, my books translated into many languages, after all of this, I was always in need of money, always just two jumps ahead of the sheriff.

"Well, I will do it. I will. I will."

For two days, three, a week, I wrote doggedly, with dogged determination.

"I will give them just what they want. I had been told, it had been impressed deeply upon my mind that, above all things, to be popular, successful, I must first of all observe the 'don'ts.'"

A friend, another American writer, came to see me. He mentioned a certain, at present, very popular woman writer.

"Boy, she is cleaning up," he said.

However it seemed that she, one who knew her trade and was safe, occasionally slipped.

It may be that here, in telling of this incident, I have got the story of what happened to the woman writer confused with many such stories I have heard.

However it lies in my mind that the writer was making, for the movies, an adaptation of a very popular novel of a past generation. In it there was a child who, eating candy before breakfast, was reproved by his mother.

"Put that stuff aside. It will ruin your health."

Something of that sort must have been written. It was unnoticed, got by. What, and with the candy people spending millions in advertising! What, the suggestion that candy could ruin the health of a child, candy called "stuff"!

My friend told some tale of a big damage suit, of indignant candy manufacturers.

"Why, there must be thousands of these 'don'ts,'" I said to myself.

"It would be better, in your story if your people be in what might be called comfortable positions in life."

I had got that sentence from someone. I wrote it out, tucked it up over my desk.

And so I wrote for a week, and there was a great sickness in me. I who had always loved the pile of clean white sheets on my desk, who had been for years obsessed with the notion that some day, by chance, I would find myself suddenly overtaken by a passion for writing and would find myself without paper, pencils, pens, or ink so that I was always stealing fountain pens and pencils from my friends, storing them away as a squirrel stores nuts, who, upon going for even a short trip away from home always put into my car enough paper to write at least five long novels, who kept bottles of ink stored in all sorts of odd places about the house, found myself suddenly hating the smell of ink.

There were the white sheets and I wanted to throw them all out of the window.

Days of this, a week. It may have gone on for two weeks. There were the days, something strangely gone out of life, and there were the nights. Why, I dare say that to those who do not write or paint or in any way work in the arts, all of this will seem nonsense indeed.

"When it comes to that," they will be saying, "our own work is not always so pleasant. Do you think it's always a joy to be a lawyer, wrangling over other people's ugly quarrels in courts, or being a doctor, always and forever with the sick, or a factory owner, with all this new unrest among workers, or a worker, getting nowhere working your life out for the profit of others?"

But there I was, having what is called literary fame. And I was no longer young. "Presently I will be old. The pen will fall from my hand. There will come the time of long afternoons sitting in the sun, or under the shade of a tree. I will no longer want to write. It may be that I will have my fill of people, their problems, the tangle of life, and will want only to look at sheep grazing on distant hillsides, to watch the waters of a stream rolling over rocks, or just follow with my aging eyes the wandering of a country road winding away among hills," I thought.

"It would be better for me to turn aside, make money now. I must. I must."

I remembered the advice always being given me when I was a young writer. "Go in for it," my friends said. At that time the movies had just become a gold mine for writers.

"Take it on for a time," my friends were saying to me. "You can change. Get yourself a stake. Make yourself secure and then, when you are quite safe, you can go abroad. Then you can write as you want to write."

"It may not have been good advice then but it is now," I said to myself. Formerly when I was writing all of my earlier books, I was very strong. I could work all day in the advertising place or in the factory I once owned. I could go home to my rooms. I took a cold plunge. Always, it seemed to me there was something that had to be washed away. When I was writing the Winesburg tales and, later, the novel, *Poor White*, I couldn't get tired, and often after working all day, wrote all night. I have never been one who can correct, fill in, rework his stories. I must try, and when I fail must throw away. Some of my best stories have been written ten or twelve times...

Perhaps I am only trying to say that the struggle in which we are engaged has no end, that we in America have, all of us, been led into a blind alley. We have always before us, we keep before us, the mythical thing we call "success," but for us there is, there can be, no success, for while this belief in the mythical thing called success remains among us, always in the minds of others about us, we shall be in danger of infection. I am trying to prove all of this to you by showing here how I, a veteran now among you, for a long time thinking myself safe from the contagion, was also taken with the disease.

--from *Sherwood Anderson's Memoirs*, "Book V, Into the Thirties, 8. The Sound of the Stream"

...There was the temptation and I knew it must be a terrible one: ...five hundred, a thousand a week.

"I will do it for a time. I will store up my money.

"When I have got rich I will be free."

"But, my dear fellow, do you not understand that the complete selling out of the imaginations of the men and women of America, by the artists, of the stage, by the artist story tellers, is completely and wholly an acceptance of harlotry?"

I had written all of this very bitterly, on a certain night in New Orleans, naming the men who had done it, some of them my personal friends. A good many of them were also radicals. They wanted, or thought they wanted, a new world. They thought that a new world could be made by depending on the economists...it was a time when the whole world was, seemingly, dominated by the economists. A new world was to arise, dominated by a new class, the proletariat. A good many of them had turned to the writing of so-called proletarian stories. It was the fashion.

"If I go to Hollywood, write there, get money by it, and if I give that money to the cause?"

"But please, what cause?"

"Why, to the overthrowing of capitalism, the making of a new and better world."

"But, don't you see that what you are doing...the suffering of the world, the most bitter suffering, does not come primarily from physical suffering. It is by the continual selling out of the imaginative lives of people that the great suffering comes. There the most bitter harm is done."

I accuse.

I accuse.

I had accused my fellow artists of America, had named names. I wrote for hours and hours, and when I had finished writing, had poured out all of the bitterness in me, brought on by the picture I had seen, I leaned back in my chair and laughed at myself.

"How can you accuse others when you yourself have not been tempted?"

Once, being in California, I had gone to Hollywood to see a friend working in one of the great studios; and as we walked through a hallway in one of the buildings, now often a row of little offices like the offices we used to sit in in the advertising agency, I saw the name of a writer I knew; the writer came out to me.

"And have they got you too?"

"No," I said, "I am just looking about."

"Well, they have not got you yet but they will get to you."

I had even written two or three times to agents in New York or Hollywood.

"Cannot you sell, to the pictures, such and such a story of mine?"

There had been no offers. I had not been tempted.

"Let us say," I remarked to myself that night in New Orleans after the outbreak of writing against others, accusations hurled on their heads, "that you had been offered...let us be generous...let us say twenty-five thousand for the best of all of your Winesburg stories, or, for that matter, for the whole series.

"Would you have turned the offer down? If you did such a thing everyone who knew of your constant need of money would call you a fool. Would you do it?"

I had to admit that I did not know and so, laughing at myself, I was compelled to tear up, to throw in the wastebasket, the thousands of words of my American "I Accuse."

You were, on that night in New Orleans, asking yourself whether you, the pure and holy one, would have the courage to turn down an offer of twenty-five thousand just to let someone sentimentalize one of your stories, twist the characters of the story about; yet now, because you are again nearly broke, because you are beginning to fear old age, and old age perhaps of poverty, you are at work doing the thing for which you were about to publicly accuse others and doing it for a few hundred dollars.

--from *Sherwood Anderson's Memoirs*, "Book V, Into the Thirties, 8. The Sound of the Stream"

...Oh, what the hell! You have chucked the attempt to be a manufacturer. You're broke and don't know where to turn.

"All right. Go to work. I'll give you a job for old time's sake."

He arose from his desk. "Look here," he said, "you know how I got to where I am. I stole an account, a big one. I was proud and glad when I did it.

"And now I have a hold of something and I can't let go. I don't know why but I can't. My pride is in some way involved.

"So let me tell you something. If you ever have a chance to steal an account, take it away from me as I have taken the Firestone account from the others here, but do not do as I did. Steal a little account, steal two or three little accounts. Do not get into the big time. Stay under the guns."

He laughed and turned away and oddly enough I did later steal two or three small accounts from him and when I did it he laughed again.

There wasn't, however, on each occasion, much joy in his laughter. He was no longer the old Bayard Barton with whom, when we were both younger, I had walked and talked on many a summer evening while we told each other of our dreams.

So I had begun again where I had left off when, with a good deal of beating of drums, I had gone off to Ohio to become a rich man. I was on a comparatively small salary, as it was a time of depression in advertising. In re-employing me, Barton had told me frankly that he did not need me. I had been compelled to accept the salary he offered. I began something that was to go on for the next ten years while I gave as little as I could to my job, continually saving myself for my writing, faking a good deal, being frank at least with my employer as to what I was doing, living as I continued to live for the next ten years in cheap rooming houses about the city. I lived on the North Side, the West Side, and the South Side. I moved restlessly from room to room.

I think it must have been at about this time I wrote a book of verses I called *Mid-American Chants* and there was in this book a good deal to be said about laughter. For I would have my readers to know that while the tale as set forth by myself here may sound rather solemn I was not solemn myself. Could it be that by acceptance of the fact of a rather unscrupulous and dishonorable quality in myself I had got a new freedom? I think I had...

--from *Sherwood Anderson's Memoirs*, "Book III, A Robin's Egg Renaissance, 2. Bayard Barton"

...I am not a hack writer in the sense that I have to depend on what I write for bread and butter, but I pay the price just the same. Eight hours a day I have paid, working as an advertising writer these last five years, while trying to save nerve force and courage enough to admit other writing. It has cost me dearly in fine moods destroyed, rare projects gone wrong because of lack of strength to get on with them, and all that sort of thing.

But why should I tell you of my woes? It is an old tale in the literary world...

--Letter to Mr. Waldo Frank, January 2, 1917, from *Letters of Sherwood Anderson*, # 4

Dear Charles: I have a thing in current *Nation** on the Negro in times of industrial depression, an article in current *Scribner's*,** and I have just written a new article for *Nation**** on the strike at Danville, Va. I seem to be getting into current things more and more, but I do not care much. My situation is a bit absurd. This winter I have had opportunity to make perhaps $3,000 by doing articles for popular magazines, but couldn't do them. It seems to me that I will have to find a way other than writing to make my living.

--Letter to Charles Bockler, November 26, 1930, #185, from *Letters of Sherwood Anderson*, #185

* "Look Out, Brown Man!" *Nation*, CXXI, 579-580 (November 26, 1930).
** "It's a Woman's Age," *Scribner's* LXXXVIII, 613-618 (December, 1930).
*** "Danville, Virginia," which was actually published in the *New Republic*, LXV, 266-268 (January 21, 1931).

One has to realize that, although there is truth in the Winesburg things, there is another big story to be done. We are no longer the old America. Those are tales of farming people. We've got a new people now. We are a growing, shifting, changing thing. Our life in our factory towns intensifies. It becomes at the same time more ugly and more intense.

God damn it, Brooks, I wish my books would sell for one reason. I want to quit working for a living and go wander for five years in our towns. I want to be a factory hand again and wander from place to place. I want my frame to unbend from the desk and to go look and listen to this new thing.

My songs are going to be widely abused and perhaps rightly. I'm a poor enough singer. But there is a song here, and it has been muffed. Masters might get it, but he has too keen a quality of hate.

It makes me ill when I think how little I get done and the years hurrying along, but I suppose we all know that sickness.

--Letter to Van Wyck Brooks, ? early April , 1918, from *Letters of Sherwood Anderson*, #28

...Well, I do wish you had freedom, and so also do I wish I had it. I shall probably have to write advertisements of oil well stocks to get money to publish my songs, but there is a kind of gigantic song in that if you can see it.

--Letter to Waldo Frank,? May,1917, from *Letters of Sherwood Anderson*, #13

...I'm afraid my *Testament** won't be all I want it to be.

I've had a bad six months, inside, and may be in for another.

In the first place, it began with money. I did not want any. I wanted to be poor, starve a little.

Then I would grow afraid that I would.

There was too much going on. Cornelia Anderson, while rather splendid in many ways, hadn't got hold of the kids. I had to try to get hold of them, learn something of their direction.

I got out of that one boy who has rather swept me off my feet. It's just straight love. He's marvelous just now. That's the one I left in Paris.

I was trying to make a home.

I went to Paris and found myself close to famous. That's just plain sickening. God knows, I hope you escape it. It's sheer nonsense without a spark of meaning...

I want to be as nice as a horse or a dog, and can't.

I've got energy. God knows, I write enough, feel enough. It's just all a whirlwind yet, though.

I went past an oats field being planted yesterday and thought, "Why in hell can't I grow with the oats in that field?"

I wanted to bury myself in the field and come up green.

--Letter to Paul Rosenfeld, April 29, 1927, from *Letters of Sherwood Anderson*, #143

A New Testament, published June, 1927.

...The one thing I detest, because it makes me feel detestable, is preaching or being wise man or seer.

The whole secret lies in the fact that it is also my problem to be "just the man, walking along, seeing, smelling." Could it not be that the more fool reputation a man gets the harder the job?

--Letter to Jerome Blum, April 25, 1924, from *Letters of Sherwood Anderson*, # 98

...As for *Marching Men*, well, you will never know with what interest I have waited for your reaction to the book. As I told you one day, I wrote it in the midst of the big readjustment in my own life. It was a theme that appealed strongly to my rather primitive nature. The beat and rhythm of the thing would come and go; a thousand outside things would flow in. I worked madly; then I threw the book away. Again and again I came back to it. In the end I had no idea as to whether it was good or bad. I only knew that the thing was out of me and I could turn to something else.

--Letter to Waldo Frank, ? September, 1917, from *Letters of Sherwood Anderson*, #16

I have had to come back to my grind here. It means working in an office eight hours a day at work in which I have no interest. Much of my energy is exhausted in that and in the effort to keep my outlook on life sweet and clear. Most of our artists give themselves up to protest and become in the end embittered and shrill. It is fortunate, however, that I have the constitution of an animal. I still rebound quickly and do manage to creep off into the world of the imagination.

Proof is read for my next book, *Winesburg, Ohio,* and it has gone to press. I expect it will be published in March. The new book*, a novel, stands still for the present. It wants two or three weeks' steady writing yet and then a week or two for cutting to shape. I wonder how and where I am to get the time for that.

I may be wrong, you know, Brother, but it seems to me that I am now ripe to do something, and I hate to see the years and the days go by in the writing of advertisements for somebody's canned tomatoes or in long days of consulting with some fellow as to how he can sell his make of ready-made clothes instead of the other fellow. I want to go up and down the great valley here seeing the towns and the people and writing of the(m) as I do not believe they have been written of.

Well, you see how it is. The modern system will pay me five thousand a year for writing the canned tomato advertisements. It doesn't want the other, or rather it thinks it doesn't want them.

From time to time I am tempted to go to some rich, dissatisfied man or woman and see if she won't give me the five thousand a year to do the other thing. However, when I think of it, I grow timid. It seems so like begging, and yet, you see, I would so like to do something real, and I know I have it in me to do something real.

I suppose my wanting to start a magazine is just a subterfuge. I don't really want to read manuscripts. I want to write. That's all I do want to do...

--Letter to Trigant Burrow, ? January, 1919, from *Letters of Sherwood Anderson,* # 38

Poor White

...I began publishing a magazine called *Commercial Democracy*, writing the entire magazine myself; I spent money circulating it by thousands of copies. I went from town to town preaching my idea of altruism in manufacturing and retailing to retail merchants. I have no doubt they thought me a little insane. All writers are perhaps hopelessly naïve. I decided to hold a great convention of retail paint dealers and hired a hall in the town. I went to an undertaker and rented several hundred chairs, got out a special edition of my magazine: I pictured hundreds of dealers coming to listen to me as I talked to them—they also were to join with me in my plan of making business altruistic. I would prove to them that I wanted nothing for my own work and they in turn would be satisfied with a small profit. We would make the purest, the best and the most wonderful paint in the world. How prices would be slashed! All the town would become suddenly beautiful in shining new coats of paint. The great day came and one man got off the train to come to my convention. I shall remember him as long as I live. He was a tall, awkward, bald and sad-faced man who owned a little general store in a town of fifty people. His little business failed the year after he came to me. He had brought with him to my convention his son, a sickly child of seven, and I remember that he had a bag of bananas in his hand. I took the man to a hotel of the town and he stayed with me for three or four days. Just why he came I shall never know, as he had read none of my literature and understood nothing of my purpose. Evidently he just wanted to go somewhere. I think that until the day I die I shall remember his long sad face and the smell of the bananas in the paper bag he carried in his hand...

--from *Sherwood Anderson's Memoirs*, "Book II, American Money, 9. Brother Earl"

Dear Robert Lovett: Your review of *Horses and Men* in *Dial* has stirred up in me anew a desire I have long had to write you a note. It would be infinitely nicer if I could talk to you.

As for the review, I have no quarrel with it of course. You have always been wholeheartedly generous with me.

However, you have written several reviews and articles after books of mine, and in all of them I have thought there was—in minor, but to me important directions—a misunderstanding of what I had aimed at and sometimes, it seemed to me, achieved.

You make a point, which you have made before, of my having sacrificed intelligence to the emotional. Is that quite sound? Can emotional surrender to a theme get anywhere without guiding intelligence?

Add to this your stricture about my taking people who "are mussed up."

Dear friend, do you really know anyone who is not mussed up?

Naturally I prefer, in life and in art, drawing close to rather sensitive people. Can a man be at all sensitive to life and be quite clear and unriled?

It would seem to me a kind of stupidity to be so.

And does not the very point you make—that one person chose a particular story as having been my best, while another is untouched by that story and deeply by another—imply that the writer of all these various tales has used his head also?

You see, I am puzzled by you, frankly.

The wide divergence of opinions you have heard are, of course, even more apparent to me. Ferdinand* and Paul Rosenfeld (two widely different types of men, I think) were both deeply moved by "An Ohio Pagan" in this book, a tale that apparently left you untouched.

You do also take for granted the failure of the novels. That seems strange to me. Both *Poor White* and *Many Marriages* seemed to me to do what I wanted them to do. One does not go from the novel to the short tale for any reason but that some themes offer themselves for long, involved treatment, others for direct, simple treatment.

You see, I am not quarreling with you, dear man. I am interested to develop from you, someday, an amplification of what is only formula, if it can be found written out in a form that will answer for such men as myself.

* Ferdinand Schevill

P.S. Perhaps after all our difference is one of technical formula. Perhaps you do have a formula on which you may depend. I wish I had. Your saying definitely that the novels are "failures" does imply, doesn't it, that you know they are?

And yet how deeply they have touched many people, how completely they have sometimes seemed to answer.

Not often, I grant you.

I certainly do not wish to be impertinent, dear Lovett, but I wish also the definite implied (*sic*) in any (ms. torn) article I have seen of yours. Perhaps I shall have to wait until some day when I can walk and talk with you. Sincerely

(P.S.) Perhaps the word "mussed" is too strong. I mean to imply that the general mess reacts on the lives of all sensitive people. That I try to make the implication of my tales.

> --Letter to Robert Moses Lovett, early March, 1924, from *Letters of Sherwood Anderson*, # 97

The young men and women are asking me questions that—if I could answer them at all—it would take a long book to answer. If I could answer them at all how wise I should be.

Everything that has to be so definitely said so falls to pieces when said. It becomes at once half a lie. There is a kind of insult in answering off-hand questions that apparently mean so much to the one who asks. If anyone actually took my answers seriously or remembered them it would be terrible.

Poets I fancy come off better at this business. They go about reading their poetry. Poetry read, and when the poet has a good voice, is a way of singing. My father was once in the show business and did a song and dance. What rotten luck that I can neither sing nor dance.

I dare say actors come off all right. Someone else has written the lines they speak. An actor when he does not make a hit can always blame the play. Playwrights should never become actors and the actor should never write a line. The alibi is one of the prime necessities of life.

There is too much pretense in this standing up, as I am doing now, and pretending to think quickly and accurately before a lot of people. How do I know I can think at all—even in a quiet place and when I am alone? Why, I am a story-teller, not a thinker.

The questioners are very insistent. They keep at me. I fire off answers. Something inside me is beginning to grow tired. In a moment I shall fly off the handle. I will give smart impertinent answers perhaps to the most sensitive of all these people.

When I was myself a young writer I once began asking questions of another and older writer and he answered me rudely, with a vulgar fling of his hand, dismissing me. It was an experience I never forgot. The questions I had asked were of such deep importance to me—just at that time in my life.

I wanted to know how to have my cake and eat it, how to write just what I pleased and yet get well paid. You see what an important question that may be to a young writer but I cannot answer it. A whole lifetime has not taught me the answer.

That is only one of the questions now being flung at me. I feel like an animal pursued by enemies. Help, I am getting groggy. Why do so many people want to be writers anyway? There is a young man in the crowd who has just the look in his eye people always have when they are about to ask an impossible question. If he asks it I shall fling my watch at his head.

Someone rescues me. He is a professor in the college and has perhaps seen the tired puzzled look in my eyes. Or perhaps he is one of the men responsible for getting me to make that particular speech and is afraid—as I am myself—that in another moment I shall betray my ignorance of all the so deadly important things I am supposed to know about and that I do not know.

I have escaped and am walking under the stars with the professor. When we are alone together we both become human. I look at him and he looks at me. We laugh a little. I have a hunch about him. It may be his hand, I suddenly see quite clearly as we walk under a street lamp, that betrays him. "Were you ever a farmer? Did you ever hold the handles of a plow?" I ask and it turns out that he was indeed once a young farmer in a county of Ohio where I also as a young man worked on a farm. "Perhaps we once plowed adjoining fields," I think but do not inquire too closely as I like the picture that now floats up into my mind. I fancy him plowing on a sloping hillside while on another hillside, across a valley, I am also plowing. It is spring. How sweet the earth smells under our feet.

And now I am at my hotel in the university town and have gone upstairs to my room. The other plowman is now lecturing every day in this university and I am going about delivering lectures about the art of writing.

"You cannot be a great man and be human. I would like to be a great man. I so detest men who think themselves important. It is so nice to be unknown, to slip quietly through streets, seeing life while remaining unseen, feeling life, yourself unseen and unknown." Dancing thoughts in my head now. Alone in my room I could make such a wonderful speech.

I am ashamed to light the light in my room at the hotel. Why am I not a praying man? It would be so helpful to pray, for wisdom let us say. "This lecturing business is so exciting and interesting. I love it.

"This lecturing business is so terrible. It makes me feel so cheap."

And now I have crawled into bed and my light is out for the night. Faces crowding up to me, lips ask questions. I float off to sleep accompanied by a sea of floating questioning faces.

But just before I sleep I think—there was that place in my lecture. By making it just a little different I shall get more of a rise out of my audiences.

It is the showman in me who comes back and who takes command just before I float off to sleep.

        --from *Sherwood Anderson's Notebook*, "When The Writer Talks"

...But I was no millionaire. I had got a few thousand as royalty on my book *Dark Laughter* and there was the hundred dollars that came every Monday from Horace Liveright.

I was intensely bothered by that. There I was. I was presumed to be a writer. "But a writer should be writing," I told myself.

And now Ball had engaged many of the neighboring hill farmers to work for me. I had built a small frame house in the valley below the hill on which my log cabin stood. It had been thrown up hastily. I thought, "When my stone house is built I'll use it as a garage."

I slept and ate down there but in the morning I arose and climbed faithfully up to my cabin on the hill. I sat at my desk by an open window and before me, stretching away, were the tops of other hills.

The hills running away into the distance were a soft blue. They were covered by forests and the trees were just coming into leaf. Here and there, on distant hillsides, were small cleared fields and men plowing. A mountain road climbed a distant hill and a man on horseback went slowly up the road.

It was all too grand. I sat in the cabin with my pen in hand and there were the blank sheets on the desk before me and down below, on Ripshin Creek, the materials for my house were being brought in.

Men were at work down there and there I was up there on that hill, my pen poised in my hand, no words coming to me.

I sprang up and went outside my cabin to look out.

"Why, I cannot write. It is too exciting down there. This is the great time in a man's life. We are all, at heart, builders. It is the dream of every man, at some time in his life, to build his own house.

"And so my house is to be built and I am to stay up here, writing words on paper. How silly."

But there was that hundred dollar check. It came every Monday morning.

Horace had said, "I will send it to you every week for five years. I'll take what you write."

"I'll not bother you," he said.

Yet each week the arrival of the check was a reminder that I was not and perhaps could not be a writer while my house was building.

"But I am under this obligation to Horace." I went again into my hilltop cabin. What really happened was that I never did write a word in that cabin. It may be that the view from the hilltop was too magnificent. It made everything I wrote seem too trivial. I had in the end, after my house was built, to move the cabin from the hill, tuck it away among the trees by the creek.

But I was still up there and down below the work on my house was under way. I had to give it up. I took a train to New York.

"Please, Horace, quit it."

"Quit what?" he asked.

"Quit sending me that money."

I tried to explain how it affected me.

"But," he said, "I have made enough on the one book—I am in the clear. Why should you worry?"

I had a hard time convincing him. He even became suspicious.

"Are you not satisfied with me as your publisher? Is that it?"

It seemed, as he said, impossible to him that a writer should refuse money.

"All right, I'll quit it, but I think that you are a little crazy."

And so I was released. It is true that, when my house was half finished, I had to go lecturing. It was bad enough but it was better than having the checks come every Monday to remind me that I was a writer, not a builder.

And this suggests something to my mind. Do you, the reader, belong to some literary circle in your town or city? Do you attend lectures by novelists and poets? Would you like to know something of the financial standing of these men and women? If so, you do not need to go to Dun and Bradstreet. If they are lecturing it is a hundred to one they are broke.

--from *Sherwood Anderson's Memoirs*, "Book IV, The Literary Life, 11. I Build A House"

...The book (i.e., *Winesburg, Ohio*—author's note) came back not only from John Lane. It came back from several other publishers. One of them, on whom I called, handed me a copy of a novel by an Anglo-American author he was then promoting. "Read this and learn how to write," said he.

Then on a Sunday, a cold wintry day, I waited on the corner of Fifty-ninth Street and the Park in New York. I had gotten a letter from Ben Huebsch, now editor-in-chief of the Viking Press, but then doing business under his own name. He wrote asking me to see him when I next came to New York, and, within a few weeks, being in New York, I phoned him. He told me where to meet him, as I understood at the Central Park corner. We were to go to a certain restaurant.

"I will meet you there at the corner at four," he had said over the phone and I think I must have been, at what I understood to be the appointed place, at three.

I stood and waited and he did not come. The hours passed. It was four o' clock, then five, then six. I am sure it will be difficult for me to make the reader understand how I felt.

It is to be borne in mind that, by this time, my stories had been rather kicked around for three or four years. I had been tender about these people of my stories, had wanted understanding and tenderness for them; and it had happened already with men on whom I had counted, that when I had shown them the stories they had rejected them.

I was there, in the city, on the Sunday afternoon, waiting on the street corner and it was cold and my heart was cold. I had got the notion that Mr. Huebsch, like so many other publishers, did not want my stories.

What a shabby trick he had played me! "Why," I asked myself, "did he need to encourage me?" As regards the particular stories there had been so much rejection, so much head shaking among my friends, that, unfairly enough, it did not occur to me that a simple mistake as regards a place of meeting had been made. I do not think that at any time later I ever told Mr. Huebsch but, on that afternoon, I certainly cursed him. I became a Nazi. "He is a Jew," I said to myself and standing there, in the city street corner on the wintry afternoon, I raised my hands to Heaven and cursed the Jews. Under the same circumstances, feeling as I did at the moment, I am sure I would have done the same for the English, the German, the Irish. I would have thought them a deceitful and tricky race.

"But why did he ask me to meet him? Is he a sadist? Did he want to torture me?" At least other publishers, to whom my book had been submitted, had been frankly cold. They had not aroused my hopes. I went back to my hotel and threw myself on the bed. It all seems very silly now but on the evening in the hotel room, with the tears flowing from my eyes...Occasionally I stopped weeping to curse, consigning all publishers to hell and reserving a special place in hell for poor Ben Huebsch...on that evening I was really more desperate than I had ever been before in my life.

And then, at last...it must have been at about nine...my telephone rang and there was Mr. Huebsch and I managed to control myself while he told me that, while I had been on one corner waiting for him he had been on another waiting for me. There had been a simple misunderstanding and, as for the book, he said that he would make no bones about that.

"Yes," he said, over the phone, "I want the book. I only wanted to meet you to talk over details," he said.

"And you do not want to tinker, to change my stories, to tell me how you think they should be written?"

I am quite sure that my voice must have trembled as I asked the question.

"You do not want to tell me that they are not stories?"

"No, of course not," he said.

--from *Sherwood Anderson's Memoirs*, "Book IV, The Literary Life, I. Waiting for Ben Huebsch"

Chapter Five

The Craft of Writing

Why is it important to take one's commitment to writing seriously?

Consider the tantalizing difference in the quality of work produced by two men. In the first we get at times an almost overwhelming sense of proficiency in his craft. The writer, we feel, knows form, knows construction, knows words. How he slings the words about. Almost every one of his lines is quotable.

And this other fellow. His words do not cling, his art forms become at times shapeless, he stumbles, going crudely and awkwardly forward.

And how breathlessly we follow. What is he doing that he holds us so tightly? What is the secret of our love of him, even in the midst of his awkwardness?

He is revealing himself to us. See how shamelessly and boldly he is trying to tell us of the thing that is a never-ceasing marvel to him—the march of his own life, the complete story of his own adventure in the midst of the universal adventure.

--from *Sherwood Anderson's Notebook*, "From Chicago, #4"

Dear Pearson*: Your fine letter stirs me. It makes me want to write you at length. There is so much to be said, and I am not now thinking of *Death in the Woods* or any of my own works, but rather of writing, or, for that matter, of the practice of any art now in our time.

I presume that we all who begin the practice of an art begin out of a great hunger for order. We want brought into consciousness something that is always there but that gets so terribly lost. I am walking on a country road, and there is a man on the hillside plowing. There is something nice, even beautiful, in the man striding at the plow handles, in the breasts of the horse pulling, in the earth rolling back from the plow, in the newly turned earth below and the sky above.

We want not only to know that beauty but to have him, at the plow handles, know.

You see, Pearson, I have the belief that in this matter of form it is largely a matter of depth of feeling. How deeply do you feel it? Feel it deeply enough, and you will be torn inside and driven on until form comes.

You spoke of the story "Hands" in *Winesburg*, and it just happens that the particular story was the first one I ever wrote that did grow into form. I remember well the thing happening. I had been struggling with it and with other stories, and at last one rainy night—I was living in a little Chicago rooming house—it came clear.

I remember the feeling of exaltation, of happiness, of walking up and down the room with tears flowing from my eyes.

It was a kind of coming out of darkness into light.

And I do not believe that, when it happens so, the feeling that comes is one of pride in achievement. For the moment form is achieved, the thing goes entirely out of you. It no longer exists in you or as a part of you. It is rather like a child, born of a woman, that begins at once to have a life of its own aside from her life.

I think this whole thing must in some way be tied up with something I can find no other word to describe aside from the word "morality." I suppose I think that the artist who doesn't struggle all his life to achieve this form, let it be form, betrays this morality. It is terribly important because, to my way of thinking, this morality may be the only true morality there is in the world.

*Norman Holmes Pearson {1909- } , professor of English at Yale.

For—and this is particularly true of the story writer—there are always others involved. The story writer is not in the position of the painter who is seeking form in nature. He brings other people into his stories.

And what is so little understood is that, in distorting the lives of these others—often imagined figures, to be sure—to achieve some tricky effect, you are betraying not only this indefinable thing we call form, but that you are betraying all of life—in short, that it is as dirty and unworthy a thing to betray these imagined figures as it would be to betray or sell out so-called real people in real life.

And so this whole matter of form involves, for the story writer, also this morality. I should think it might very well be made the whole point of the introduction for your book. It is the thing so terribly important to every artist.

And it may well be that, in some way, it is just this artist's point of view, this morality, always to be gone toward, and that occasionally forces him to bring his materials into real form, that is the only thing that may, in the end, pull mankind out of its mess. Sincerely

--Letter to Norman Holmes Pearson, after September 13, 1937, from *Letters of Sherwood Anderson*, # 322

I want constantly to push out into experimental fields. "What can be done in prose that has not been done?" I keep asking myself.

And so I constantly set out on new roads.

What is gained? --perhaps nothing but a little colorful strength in my everyday writing. I push on, knowing that no one will perhaps care in the least for these experiments into which I put so much emotion (al) force.

It is at least the adventure.

--Letter to Van Wyck Brooks, March 31, 1919, from *Letters of Sherwood Anderson*, # 39

Hackett[1] always attacks me by saying my sense of form is atrocious, and it may be true. However, he also commends me for getting a certain large, loose sense of life. I often wonder, if I wrapped my packages up more neatly, if the same large, loose sense of life could be attained.

This has been an amusing year. Neither *Poor White* (n)or *Winesburg* were selling much until W.L. George[2] and later Sinclair Lewis began talking about me. Now they do sell, not hugely, but surprisingly well for me. In other words, I find people taking these two fellows' word on me as an artist. The gods must be amused. Lists of names float through the papers. I am at various times grouped with Fitzgerald of *This Side (of) Paradise*[3], Webster[4], William Allen White[5], Dell[6], Lewis, E.P. Roe[7] and others.

In the matter of form, Paul, I have much to say to you that we shall have an opportunity to say this summer. One thing I would like you to know is this: as far as I am concerned, I can accept no standard I have ever seen as to form. What I most want is to be and remain always an experimenter, an adventurer. If America could have the foolish thing sometimes spoken of as "Artistic Maturity" through me, then America could go to the devil.

I am not so foolish as to think of this statement as in any way a challenge to you and your point of view; it is rather an assurance to you that the praise I may have had this year does for the most part seem utterly foolish to me.

--Letter to Paul Rosenfeld, March 10, 1921, from *Letters of Sherwood Anderson*, #59

[1] Francis Hackett.
[2] W.L. George (1882-1926), novelist, whose *A Bed of Roses* (1911) was an 'emancipated' treatment of prostitution.
[3] Published 1920.
[4] Henry Kitchell Webster (1875-1932), who published *Real Life* in 1921.
[5] William Allen White (1868-1944), novelist, editor of the *Emporia Gazette* after 1895.
[6] Floyd Dell published *The Briary Bush* in 1921.
[7] Edward Payson Roe (1838-1888), author of *Barriers Burned Away* (1872), *Opening a Chestnut Burr* (1874), and other sentimental novels.

It is odd what literary connections one makes. In my own mind I have always coupled Mark Twain with George Borrow*. I get the same quality of honesty in them, the same wholesome disregard of literary precedent.

--Letter to Van Wyck Brooks, Chicago, early April, 1918, from *Letters of Sherwood Anderson*, #28

*The English novelist (1803-1881), author of *Lavengro* and *The Romany Rye*, was one of Anderson's favorite authors.

It was in Chicago that I first knew other writers and men deeply interested in literature. I had come back to my big town to try again. I was living about in cheap rooming houses trying to get some ground under my feet, to give my own life some decent purpose and meaning, growing often discouraged and going with others to carouse in so-called low saloons. And here in Chicago I wrote many of my best-known stories. It was in Chicago that the newspapers first both damned and praised my work...*

There I saw the first woman who rejected me—felt what men feel when they are so rejected. There I first made ink flow, sang my first song. There after many efforts I wrote a sentence I could bear reading the next day.**

--*from *Sherwood Anderson's Memoirs*, "Book III, A Robin's Egg Renaissance, 1. The Nest"

--**from *Sherwood Anderson's Memoirs*, "Book II, American Money, 1. Chicago"

...We spoke certain words and thought others. Often things hung in the balance. A word from her or from me would have opened up vast reservoirs of possibilities in our relations.

When I was younger, stronger, and perhaps more foolish, I used to think it would be well if everyone spoke their hidden thoughts aloud. Later I grew away from that notion. No one is good enough, strong enough, rich enough.

What I have just now been writing related to work, that is to say to writing, singing, dancing, painting, is difficult to say in words.

The relation you seek always exists. The rhythm you are seeking in any of the arts lies just below the surface of things in nature. To get below the surface, to get the lower rhythm into your hands, your body, your mind, is what you seek but having achieved it you are soon exhausted. It is necessary to come back to the surface, to be like a tree or a field. Men who can work at any time in any art have no relation to their art at all. Their relation to their work has no more reality than the giving of her body by a prostitute has to do with the reality of love.

--from *Sherwood Anderson's Notebook*, "Notes Out of a Man's Life, Note 19"

I know that you have often been puzzled by a certain attitude in me. You have several times said that you thought I might make a great deal of money by my trade. You have seemed to think me foolish for not trying to do it.

But there's the rub. In my trade the money is made by giving the life you represent in your writing a certain twist—glamor is the word. It seems to me to be but creating new misunderstandings, like the illusion always being built up that there is happiness in getting rich. Occasionally you meet a rich man. Well, he is no more happy than you or I.

Sometimes I think, Andy, that the artist is the only religious man we have left. There was once a kind of religion in good honest work in workingmen, but it has been hurt, destroyed by modern high speed industry. We get cheap chairs, tables, suits of clothes, etc., but with them get a cheapened kind of man. As workman you can't work, day after day, making, for example (cheap articles)* without growing immoral. We lose sense of the value of morality, the kind of morality, for example, that makes us so respect an Abraham Lincoln.

We are all, you see, constantly being rule(d) by a force that i(s) not at all physical. We have imaginations. Nearly all of our intercourse with each other is through the imagination. If I take you as a friend, it is because you help feed my imagination. If I get high on some woman, it is because she does that or because I can exercise my own imagination by courting her. The trouble is that so few of us ever get trained imaginations. We play with the imagination like children playing with toys.

The false artist is always putting a false glamor over life. He betrays our imaginations. It is really the great betrayal, and it is being done all the time, in the movies, in the theater, in books and stories, over the radio. It is one of the things that ha(s) most to do with our loneliness, our separation from each other. It does it by killing any real understanding.

--Letter to Charles H. Funk, October 30, 1938, from
Letters of Sherwood Anderson, # 349

*Seven words have been deleted by the editors and the two in brackets inserted by them to indicate the general sense of the deleted material.

...I was in one of my frightened moods. Soon now my money would all be gone. I am a man who has always had, in the matter of finance, a line that, when crossed, made me begin to tremble. Anything above five hundred dollars in the bank has always seemed to me riches, but when my bank account goes below that amount the fears come.

Soon I shall have but four hundred dollars, then three, then two, one. I live in the country on a farm and in the house built by my one successful book. Bills come, so many pounds of grass seed for a field, a ton of lime, a new plow. Great God, will I be compelled to return to the advertising agency?

I have three or four short stories in my agent's hands. Once a magazine called *Pictorial Review* paid me seven hundred and fifty dollars for a short story. I had given the story the title, "There She is, She is Taking Her Bath," but after the story had been got into type and illustrations made for it the editor of the magazine grew doubtful. "We are doubtful about the title," he wired. "Can't you suggest another?" and I replied, saying, "ROLL YOUR OWN," but got from him a second wire, saying that he didn't think that that title fitted the story and in the end he never published it.

"Will he be demanding back my seven hundred and fifty dollars?" I asked myself, knowing nothing of my legal rights. But then a thought came, a very comforting thought.

"He may demand but how can he get it?" I had spent the money for an automobile, had got a new overcoat, a new suit of clothes.

"Just let him try. What can he do? I am dustproof," I muttered; but I had misjudged the man. He must really have been a splendid fellow, for in the end and without protest, and after some four or five years, he sent the story back to me saying nothing at all of all that money given me for it. He said, if I remember correctly, that, while he personally liked the story, in fact thought it splendid, a magnificent achievement, etc., etc., also that he had always greatly admired my work, this story did not really fit into the tone of the magazine. There was in it, as I now remember, a little business man, timid and absurdly jealous of his wife. He had got it into his head that she was having affairs with other men and had determined to have it out with her but, when he worked himself up to it and rushed home, always fearing he would lose his courage, it happened that invariably she was taking her bath. A man couldn't, of course, stand outside the door of the bathroom, his wife splashing in the tub, and through the door accuse her of unfaithfulness.

In my story the wife was, to be sure, quite innocent. As a detective he hired to watch her assured him, she was as innocent as a little flower...if I remember correctly that was the expression used...but, also, as in so many of my stories, there was a business man made to appear a little ridiculous.

Why, I am told there are men and women who receive, for a single short story, as much as a thousand, fifteen hundred, even two thousand dollars. I am also told that I have had a profound effect upon the art of short- story writing.

"And so, what's wrong?" I more than a hundred times have asked myself; but at last I have come to a conclusion.

"You are just a little too apt, Sherwood, my boy, to find the business man a little ridiculous," I have told myself.

"Yes, and there is just your trouble, my boy. The business man, as he is represented in our picture, as he must be represented, is, above all things, a shrewd and knowing man. It would be better to represent him as very resolute, very courageous. He should have really what is called 'an iron jaw.' This is to indicate resolution, courage, determination.

"And you are to bear in mind that earlier in life he was an athlete. He was a star football player, a triple threat, whatever that is, or he was one of the team at Yale.

"He is older now but he has kept himself in trim. He is like the first Roosevelt, the Teddy one. Every day he goes to his club to box. The man who is to succeed in business cannot...keep that in mind...let himself grow fat. Do not ever make him fat, watery-eyed, bald. Do not let him have a kidney complaint."

"The trouble with you," I told myself, "is just the years you spent in business," and I began to remember the men, hundreds of them, some of them known internationally, often sensitive fellows, at bottom kindly, who were puzzled as I was puzzled, always breaking out into odd confessions, telling intimate little stories of their loves, their hopes, their disappointments.

"How did I get where I am? What brought me here?"

"This is something I never wanted to do. Why am I doing it?"

Something of that sort and then also, so often, something naïve, often wistful and also a little ridiculous.

I could not shake off the fact that, in the fifteen or twenty years during which I was in business as advertising writer, as manufacturer, five men among my personal acquaintances killed themselves.

So there was tragedy too, plenty of it.

"But, my dear fellow, you must bear in mind that this is a country ruled by business. Only yesterday, when you were driving on the highway, you saw a huge sign. 'What is good for business is good for you,' the sign said.

"So there, you see, we are one great brotherhood."

All of this said to myself, over and over. "Now you are below the line, the five-hundred-dollar line. Keep that in mind."

There were these days, my struggle to write in a new vein, to keep persistently cheerful, letting nothing reflecting on the uprightness, the good intent, the underlying courage of business, creep into my story.

"Above all do not put into your story a business man who is by chance shy, sensitive, who does occasionally ridiculous things. Even if, at bottom, the fellow is gentle, lovable, do not do that."

"But, you see, my man is not in business. I have made him a judge.

"But, you fool, don't you see...my God, man, a judge.

"Is there not also a pattern, a mold made, for the judge?"

And so you see me arguing, fighting with myself, through the days, through the nights. The nights were the worst.

"But can't you sleep, my dear?"

"No, my darling, I cannot sleep."

"But what is on your mind?"

You see, I cannot tell my wife. She would rebel. She would begin talking about a job. "We can give up this house, this farm," she would say. "You are always spending your money on it," she would add. She would call attention to the absurd notion I have that, in the end, I can make our farm pay. We would get into an argument, with me pointing out that it is a dishonorable thing to live on land and not work constantly to make it more productive.

"It would be better for me to surrender everything else before my love of the land itself," I would say, and this would set me off. As she is a Southern woman I would begin on the South, pointing out to her how the masters of the land and the slaves of the old South, claiming as they did an aristocratic outlook on life, had been, nevertheless, great land destroyers; and from that I would go on, declaring that no man could make claim to aristocracy who destroyed the land under his feet.

It is a favorite subject of mine and it gets us nowhere.

"I think I have been smoking too many cigarettes," I said and she agreed with me. She spoke again, as she had so often, of her fear of the habit-forming danger of a certain drug I sometimes take; but—"You had better take one," she said.

And so I did but it did not help.

"But why should you be afraid?" I asked myself. Even after I had taken the drug I was wide awake and remained so night after night.

But why go on? We story tellers, and I am writing all of this solely for story tellers, all know, we must know, it is the beginning of knowledge of our craft, that the unreal is more real than the real, that there is no real other than the unreal; and I say this here because, first of all, I presume to re-establish my own faith—badly shaken recently by an experience—and I say it a little because as a veteran story teller I want to strengthen the faith in other and younger American men.

--from *Sherwood Anderson's Memoirs*, "Book V, Into the Thirties, 8. The Sound of the Stream"

I had put a fellow novelist into one of my books. In a certain situation he had failed to draw the line and I said so.

He came to visit me. His personal life was also involved and difficult. When I saw the position into which he had got himself by failing to draw the line in life, as he had failed to draw it in the fanciful life of his books, I took out of my book the brutal note in the reference to him.

It is all very well to call a man names who can get even with you but it is dreadful when you know he can't.

--from *Sherwood Anderson's Notebook*, "Notes Out of a Man's Life, Note 22"

I dare say what I had thought of the art of writing, when I had thought of it at all, was that at bottom it was very much like paint making, or like running an advertising agency. You did it to make money.

To be sure, to do it at all you had to have, born in you, perhaps a certain kind of talent.

For example to be a real story teller. I rather think I always was one. You see this experience with the man Luther (See page 74 --author's note) must be thought of also as a growing thing, my being more and more with the man, sensing things in him. Let us think of it as a kind of love making on his part. And I do not mean a physical love making.

But he had got hold of something in me. When we were together we did not always talk seriously. Sometimes he spoke of nothing but the art of printing. He had a passion for certain fine papers and for certain fonts of type, and would sometimes run clear across town to my office to show me a page. "Look. Isn't it beautiful?"

It may have been. I did not know. This matter of the surface of things in life, the shape of an apple or a pear hanging on a tree, the tree, the bed you sleep in, the chair you sit in.

The effect of a room on an inner thing in yourself. All of this was, I think, at that time, rather Greek to me...

And here let me say something to those who are beginners in the arts. It is a slow painful process, this training the senses toward the more subtle things of life, toward something of getting, or at least beginning to get, some sense of the real beauty of life in its physical aspects. Why I, who now have rather trained faculties in this direction, when I began...I thought many things beautiful that I now think ugly. I think it must have been under Luther's influence that I began...in the matter of pictures for example. I got a scrap book and kept it in my room. "This man has something I am going to get," I said with determination and so I kept the scrap book and began cutting drawings out of magazines. I pasted the drawings in the book and sat thumbing it. Occasionally I took it to Luther.

He was polite. I can see his eyes yet, looking at my book, and I can hear his polite words. "Very nice. Some of them are quite nice." It was like a man speaking to a child.

--from *Sherwood Anderson's Memoirs*, "Book II, American Money, 8. The Man of Ideas"

...But, dear man, you do so make the world a living place for so many people. I imagine only a few have really got to know you. It takes time and a kind of power in oneself to know another just as it does to get anywhere in one of the crafts. There are little distracting things not understood in oneself and the other. As for myself, I freely admit that I have often been stupid about you, and it was only last year that I came to know and really value you.

One day I was going to the country, and as I sat in the train, I suddenly began to weep bitterly and had to turn my face away from the people in the car for shame of my apparent(ly) causeless grief. However, I was not unhappy. It was just that I had at last realized fully what your life had come to mean to me. In our age, you know, there is much to distract from the faithful devotion to cleanliness and health in one's attitude toward the crafts, and it takes time to realize what the quality has meant in you. I really think, man, you have registered more deeply than you know on Marin*, O'Keeffe, Rosenfeld, myself and others...

You have kept the old faith that gets so lost and faint, but that always has some man like yourself to make it real again to the younger ones. At any rate, you may know that this feeling I have come to have for you is no sudden thing, but a slow, sure growth...

--Letter to Alfred Stieglitz, June 10, 1923, from *Letters of Sherwood Anderson*, #79

*John Marin (1872-), whose work was often exhibited at "291."

But why, I am constantly asked, is crudity and ugliness necessary? Why cannot a man like Mr. Dreiser write in the spirit of the early Americans, why cannot he see fun in life? What we want is the note of health. In the work of Mark Twain there was something wholesome and sweet. Why cannot the modern man be also wholesome and sweet?

To this I make answer that to me a man, say like Mr. Dreiser, is wholesome. He is true to something in the life about him and truth is always wholesome. Twain and Whitman wrote out of another age, out of an age and a land of forests and rivers. The dominant note of American life in their time was the noisy swaggering raftsman and the hairy-breasted woodsman. Today it is not so. The dominant note in American life today is the factory hand. When we have digested that fact, we can begin to approach the task of the present-day novelist with a new point of view.

It is, I believe, self-evident that the work of the novelist must always lie somewhat outside the field of philosophic thought. Your true novelist is a man gone a little mad with the life of his time. As he goes through life he lives, not in himself, but in many people. Through his brain marches figures and groups of figures. Out of the many figures one emerges. If he be at all sensitive to the life about him and that life be crude the figure that emerges will be crude and will crudely express itself.

I do not know how far a man may go on the road of subjective writing. The matter, I admit, puzzles me. There is something approaching insanity in the very idea of sinking yourself too deeply into modern American industrial life.

But it is my contention that there is no other road. If a man would avoid neat slick writing he must at least attempt to be brother to his brothers and live as the men of his time live. He must share with them the crude expression of their lives. To our grandchildren the privilege of attempting to produce a school of American writing that has more delicacy and color may come as a matter of course. I hope that will be true but it is not true now. And that is why, with so many of the younger Americans, I put my faith in the modern literary adventurers. We shall, I am sure, have much crude blundering American writing before the gift of beauty and subtlety in prose shall honestly belong to us.

--from *Sherwood Anderson's Notebook*, "An Apology For Crudity"

...When I had left my factory, walking down the railroad tracks that day in 1910, I had kept on walking until I got to the city of Cleveland. It was summer and I slept for two nights out of doors. One night in a lumber yard and another night in an open field. In Cleveland I had borrowed a little money from a friend, Mr. Edwin Baxter, now I believe an official in one of Cleveland's larger banks, and had returned to Chicago. The days and nights of walking and of lying out under the sky had been a time of soul wrestling. I had come to a certain conclusion. "I cannot change American life," I told myself. "It is not in me to be a leader of men leading them into new paths." I already knew that when I returned to Chicago there would be but one fate open to me. I could again become an advertising writer. Essentially as an advertising writer I would continue indulging in lies. I had a gift for words, a gift of statement. Deep within me somewhere there was a respect for words. I would be compelled, as advertising writer, to corrupt these words. They were the instruments by which possibly men might find each other in the confusion of life. "Very well," I said to myself, "I will stick to those dependent upon me. I will be corrupt but, God give me this grace," I cried, "let me in some way keep an honest mind. When I am being corrupt, perverting the speech of men, let me remain aware of what I am doing." I dare say that many times later I either lost this impulse or became confused about it but I always returned to it. It seemed to me then, as it does now, that hypocrisy in this matter, this believing your own bunk, was the real sin against the Holy Ghost. As writer I believe it yet. I have nothing, for example, to say against the American writer who flies off to Hollywood and gets his thousand a week for what must be done to get the thousand a week in Hollywood, except when I hear such a one talking, as they are always doing, about the wonderful possibilities of the movies and trying to convince themselves that they are not being corrupt. With a few exceptions, the movies, as I have seen them, have done nothing to improve the relationship between man and man in America or to make our common lives more understandable.

It was the advertising agency which formerly had employed me that, after some hesitation, had taken me back.

"I do hope you'll go straight now."

This would have been Bayard Barton, who had now become president of the agency, talking to me. Bayard was too gentle a man to be really gruff.

"And what do you mean by going straight?"

The conversation would have taken place in his office.

"Well, Bayard, you have certainly risen in the world." He had been a copy writer as I had been. We had sat together in the same little hall of a room, writing of cough cures, fertilizers for farms, rouge for women's cheeks.

I had something on Bayard. Did he not formerly show me verses he had written?

And now he was lecturing me. It was an old story. From my own wife I had got just such lectures.

"It is about this scribbling of yours. You cannot have such divided interests. Either you are an advertising man or you are a writer."

"Yes, I know," I said. "You are about to speak now of my lack of education. Such men as myself, who are not college men, whose minds have not been disciplined, cannot become real writers.

"I have heard all of that, have heard it to weariness, but I do not see that what I do after hours, when I am not employed here in this office, can matter to you."

Bayard would have called my attention to my failure as a manufacturer.

"It was because your real interest was not in the business.

"And then besides I know well that in coming back here you are only coming back because you are broke.

"You have no interest in advertising writing. In a month you will be swaggering before us, your tongue in your cheek."

"And writing darn good copy for you," I said, laughing at him. For well I knew he would not turn me down. There was something between us, a kind of affection.

And had he not also once said to me that, when he had made his pile...that an old dream.--No man or woman among us doing what he wanted to do. We were writing, dreaming, hoping.

"When I make my pile."

Among us writers the dream of writing for the popular magazines or the so-called "pulps," or, if more lucky, getting a script job in Hollywood. Big money to be made and put aside. Then some real work done.

It didn't seem to work out.

I sat looking at Bayard who was looking at me. There was a silence between us. We were both thinking of former days, when we had both been copy writers together, walks taken in the evening, talks we had.

"There is so much whoredom. I wonder if it is possible to escape it. All of this spending our lives struggling to get a little ahead of the other fellow, make more money. It is a disease of our civilization."

--from *Sherwood Anderson's Memoirs*, "Book III, A Robin's Egg Renaissance, 2. Bayard Barton"

...May I say that until I found the Russian writers of prose, your Tolstoy, Dostoevski, Turgenev, Chekhov, I had never found a prose that satisfied me. In America we have had a bad tradition, got from the English and the French. To our tales that are popular in our magazines one goes for very clever plots, all sorts of trickery and juggling. The natural result is that human life becomes secondary, of no importance. The plot does not grow out of the natural drama resulting from the tangle of human relations, whereas in your Russian writers one feels life everywhere, in every page.

I remember how, as a boy, I heard of Russia as a strange, cruel land in which—one got the notion—well, you see, it was a land in which most of the people spent their lives down in dark mines. A few tall figures in beards and wearing expensive fur coats strode about. Everyone carried a whip with which to beat others.

I had this picture, and then I came to your writers. A door opened. I saw at last that the art of prose writing might spring into life directly out of an impulse of sympathy and understanding with the man beside you.

Is it not possible that your people think of us Americans also as giants going about jingling dollars, piling up great heaps of dollars in the streets? One day last year a young Russian who lives in Chicago now walked with me in one of the crowded, noisy streets there. "It does not want a new land and a new people here. It wants Dostoevski or a Tolstoy to come into this street and see things with their eyes," he said.

We are a mixed people, all races thrown together. Our cities are ugly. We have not come to such an understanding of each other as might come readily if we were all one people, but we Americans are men and women too.

If my tales or novels make you feel that, I shall be glad. Very sincerely yours

--Letter to Peter Ochremenko*, January, 1923, from
Letters of Sherwood Anderson, #73

*Russian translator then working for the All-Russian State Publishing Company

What dreams, hopes, ambitions. Sometimes it had seemed to me, when as a young man I sat at the window of that room, that each person who passed along the street below, under the light, shouted his secret up to me.

I was myself and still I fled out of myself. It seemed to me that I went into the others.

What dreams. What egotism. I had thought, on such evenings, that I could tell all of the stories of all the people of America. I would get them all, understand them, get their stories told.

And then the night came when it happened.

But what happened? It is the thing so hard to explain. It is, however, the thing every young man and woman in the world will understand.

I had been working so long, so long. Oh, how many thousand, hundreds of thousands of words put down.

Trying for something.

To escape out of old minds, old thoughts put into my head by others, into my own thoughts, my own feelings.

Out of the others, the many, many others, who had worked in words, to have got so much I wanted but to be freed from them.

To at last go out of myself, truly into others, the others I met constantly in the streets of the city, in the office where I then worked, and still others, remembered out of my childhood in an American small town.

To be myself, and yet at the same time the others.

And then, on a day, late in the afternoon of a day, I had come home to that room. I sat at a table in a corner of the room. I wrote.

There was a story of another human, quite outside myself, truly told.

The story was one called "Hands." It was about a poor little man, beaten, pounded, frightened by the world in which he lived into something oddly beautiful.

The story was written that night in one sitting. No word of it ever changed. I wrote the story and got up. I walked up and down in that little narrow room. Tears flowed from my eyes.

"It is solid," I said to myself. "It is like a rock. It is there. It is put down."

There was, I'm sure, an upsurge of pride.

"See, at last I have done it.

"It is true. There it is."

In those words, scrawled on the sheet of paper, it is accomplished.

I am quite sure that on that night, when it happened in that room, when for the first time I dared whisper to myself, perhaps sobbing, that I had found it, my vocation, I knelt in the darkness and muttered words of gratitude to God.

That I had been on the right track, that I dared hope.

Pride, exaltation, all mixed with a new and great humbleness.

"It happened in that room.

"There I found my vocation..

"It is what we all want.

"All of this frantic search for wealth, for fame, position in life—it is all nothing.

"What we want, every one of us, is our own vocation.

"It is the world hunger."

Those words going through my mind as I stood at the door of a shabby room in a shabby rooming house years later with my wife.

Remembering all my failures since that night when I, alone there in that room, found for the first time my own vocation.

Getting for the first time belief in self.

I must have muttered words to the landlady, taken my wife's arm, hurried out of that house, feeling deeply the shame of my many failures since that, the greatest moment of my life.

When I found what every man and woman in the world wants.

A vocation.

--from *Sherwood Anderson's Memoirs*, "Book III, A Robin's Egg Renaissance, 11. The Finding"

...I came among artists hoping to find brotherhood there, but there isn't much of it. As it is in painting, so it is among writers. Fundamentally most of our American writing men are graceful and facile fanner(s)* and whores altogether. If one did not laugh at them, he would go mad. The artisan and the mechanic talks with fair intelligence of his tools. The average professional intellectual talks, of course, like a silly, puzzled child...

--Letter to Karl Anderson**, ? November, 1917, from
Letters of Sherwood Anderson, #20

*That is, unscrupulous men.
**Karl Anderson (1874-), painter, was Sherwood's brother and the oldest of the Anderson children. See Books I and II of the *Memoirs*.

I am a great child, Waldo. You see, for all those years I worked away in the midst of laborers and businessmen and knew no artists. I had some sort of general notion that someday I should come into acquaintanceship with men at work in the arts and find them fine, generous, openhanded, ready to understand that although my art might be a poor, blundering thing, my impulses were O.K.

And then when my first book was published, an odd thing happened. People I had long known and who had looked upon me with indifferent tolerance or even friendliness praised me openly, but in secret did things to hurt me.

There has been a good deal of this sort of thing, and I haven't understood it. It has made me a little draw back into my shell. It has opened up to me the fact that men in the arts can be very small and petty. The thing had a sobering effect upon me.

And then there has been something else. I have always thought of myself as peculiarly wind-blown, a man approaching the bucolic in my nature. You know how I have had the notion that nothing from my pen should be published that could not be read aloud in the presence of a cornfield.

And many people have written me of what they call the "morbidity" of my work. It has been puzzling and confusing. I have stood like a beast pestered by flies and by the hot sun, turning my head here and there and having many disquieting little thoughts.

--Letter to Waldo Frank, before November 7, 1917, from *Letters of Sherwood Anderson,* #21

About his friend Gertrude Stein:

That her materials are the words of our English speech and that we do not, most of us, know or care too much what she is up to does not greatly matter to me. The impression I wish now to give you of her is one of very intent and earnest in a matter most of us have forgotten. She is laying word against word, relating sound to sound, feeling for the taste, the smell, the rhythm of the individual word. She is attempting to do something for the writers of our English speech that may be better understood after a time, and she is not in a hurry.

And I have always that picture of the woman in the great kitchen of words, standing there by a table, clean, strong, with red cheeks and sturdy legs, always quietly and smilingly at work. If her smile has in it something of the mystery, to the male at least, of the Mona Lisa, I remember that the women in the kitchens on the wintry mornings wore often that same smile.

She is making new, strange and to my ears sweet combinations of words. As an American writer I admire her because she, in her person, represents something sweet and healthy in our American life, and because I have a kind of undying faith that what she is up to in her word kitchen in Paris is of more importance to writers of English than the work of many of our more easily understood and more widely accepted word artists.

--from *Sherwood Anderson's Notebook*, "Four American Impressions"

Now as to your questions—I think the best way for a person, such as yourself, who desires to write, is simply to keep your eyes and ears open and learn as much about the way people live and the impulses back of their actions as you can. Keep on writing all the time and do not be discouraged if you do not write anything very good for a long time.

The question as to what authors to read is a large order, but I would as far as possible, read old authors whose work has stood the test of time, and read a great deal of history and biography.

Your third question—what is my personal favorite among my own books?--is too much like asking a mother which is her favorite child. They are to me somewhat different from what they are to the public, and I simply can't answer the question.

--Letter to Mr. Jay L. Bradley*, October 2, 1925, from *Letters of Sherwood Anderson*, # 122

*In his letter Jay Bradley identifies himself as a fifteen-year-old boy who admires Anderson's work and who wants to know how to become a writer.

It isn't my way, of course, all of these strange, jeweled adjectives. I want my own prose to go like great waves washing the sides of ships, like the Mississippi going down to the sea. It never does, but that is what I want.

--Letter to Paul Rosenfeld, ? December,1926, from *Letters of Sherwood Anderson*, #137

I have, almost always, tried to work out of pure feeling, having the conviction that if I got the feeling straight and pure enough, the form I wanted would follow.

--Letter to Maxwell Perkins, November 8, 1935, from *Letters of Sherwood Anderson*, # 269

I don't think I have ever talked to you very seriously about this, as I always took your statement that you were interested in writing rather as bunk. If you had been really interested, as you are, for example, in bird hunting, you would have been seeking and reading good work. I think that you look toward writing sometimes as an easy way to make some money—an utterly false notion. I lectured about this, that is to say, this false notion, twice at Columbia this fall and am to speak on it in Chicago in January.

I don't know how to put it to you. Writing, or any art for that matter, concerns the world of the imagination. Few enough people realize the importance of that world. I think perhaps I could explain it in this way. You also are always living in imagination. The artist tries to bring this world over into life.

But you can betray, sell out, the imaginative world as you can the real world, be false to it. This should be elaborated, and I haven't time.

You see, however, what our writers do—build up the idea, in fiction, that to be rich, have success, etc., is happiness. They pervert all the channels of existence. Look at how deeply the false idea that success was the result of merit was built up, whereas any sensible man knows that success, in the money-making sense, is almost always due to the overdevelopment of the acquisitive instinct, to trickery, and often to sheer luck.

Well enough. This endeth the first lesson.

--Letter to Charles H. Funk, ? November, 1935, from
Letters of Sherwood Anderson, #270

Whenever a new writer begins to come a little into prominence in the literary world the critics do strange things to him.

First of all they overpraise him. It is understandable enough. It is a boring job, this sitting at a desk, day after day, reading and passing judgment on other men's work.

Think, for example, of the man who become the literary critic for a daily newspaper. Some of them actually write of a new book every day.

To be sure it doesn't take long to pass on most books. You pick the book up, read a page, five pages, ten pages. It doesn't take much reading to find out whether or not a writer can write. A bit of originality, a flair for words—you are not asking too much. That curious inexplainable thing, the hidden music in prose, the overtone, the quality in real writing that sets your imagination flying off on a journey of its own, you'll not find that appearing very often.

The critic is fed up on commonplace books. A book comes that is a little alive. It is good story telling.

You cannot blame the critic if he throws his hat into the air, begins to shout.

Very likely he overdoes it. When my own first novel was published I was compared in the *New York Times* to Dostoievsky.

"An American Dostoievsky," something of that sort.

To be sure I liked it but, at the same time, it made me secretly ashamed. The book, I felt, didn't come off. I felt that the book was largely a result of my reading of other novelists. I hadn't as yet turned directly to the life about me. It was an immature book, not completely felt, full of holes and bad spots. In a later edition of the same book I rewrote the whole later part of it.

There was an upward and onward note in all the early pages of the book, a boy, coming out of an Iowa corn-shipping town to rise in the business world, that fitted into the American mood of the day. I had not got the slant on business I got later.

The book sold well. It was praised by many critics. They did not like the ending but neither did I.

I had made my man, who had risen a little in the world of affairs, come to a place where he had begun to feel sharply the futility of his life.

I didn't know what to do with him...

...It all resulted in my taking a trip to Philadelphia, where I had a talk with Mr. Curtis and was offered a position as an editorial writer for the *Saturday Evening Post*, a position I did not accept.

Just why I did not accept I did not at that time know. The Curtis Publishing Company was so big. It may have a little terrified me.

Or perhaps already I had begun to be a little afraid of all bigness, didn't want to be a big shot.

I had that chance and lost it and then came another. I had published my first novel, the one spoken of above, and a man from the Curtis office came to see me.

It was a Sunday morning and I went to meet the man at the Blackstone Hotel. We were in a room at the hotel.

"We want novels, such as you started to write when you wrote *Windy McPherson's Son*.

"We can pay well for what we want.

"We felt that the last part of the novel wasn't what we wanted.

"In all the first part of your novel there is a fresh note. As for the later part, the ending--

"In such novels that can of course be corrected.

"We feel you stumbled there."

"Yes," I said, "I guess I did."

It was what interested me, that stumbling.

I was trying to think and feel my way through a man's life. I wanted it to come to some satisfactory end for him as I would like my own life to come to some satisfactory end.

I think that, on that morning, in the hotel room, I tried to explain. Now that I think of it, there were, I'm sure, two men present from the Curtis house. I had got into the writing of novels and stories in a curious way. I had not begun by thinking of myself as a writer. I do not yet think of myself so. There is something of the eternal amateur in me. I wanted if I could to clear up certain traits in myself.

I had discovered something. I had discovered that I could, in writing, throw an imagined figure against a background of some of my own experiences—a thing all writers must do—and through the imagined figure get sometimes a kind of slant on some of my own questionable actions.

I doubt that it ever reformed me. It did give me a certain satisfaction.

I was there in the room with the two men from the house of Curtis. I tried to explain. No doubt I made a mess of it. I do not think I made them understand what I was driving at.

"But we can pay well. We pay for what we want."

It was true, and how I wanted money.

"Do you play golf?"

The two men both said that they did.

"You enjoy doing it just for the sake of doing it, not for money."

You see how confusing this is. I am always crabbing at my publishers because they do not make more money for me.

> --from *Sherwood Anderson's Memoirs*, "Book III, A Robin's Egg Renaissance, 9. A Chance Missed"

And do I want in any case to write about this apparent life of my own? When one writes of self one inevitably makes a hero of self. No, I want to use my own life only as a kind of springboard. What difference when I was born, what women I made love to, what friends I betrayed? What is interesting is the woman loved, the friend betrayed, the friend to whom I was loyal. My ambition to become rich, to be a big man as we in our town thought of big men when I was a boy, that is to say, a money maker, did pass: I became interested in people—and I want to make my book, my rambling house of a book, a book of people.

But here is something I must also explain. It happens that I have met, in the course of the life I just have briefly outlined, a good many so-called "notable" men and women, famous writers, painters, singers, actors, publishers. Whom have I not met? I have remained a restless man, ever on the move. As writer, I came into writing at a time when new paths were being made. Often nowadays my name is coupled with that of Theodore Dreiser, Sinclair Lewis, Edgar Lee Masters, Carl Sandburg, Eugene O'Neill and others as, shall I say, a "pioneer"? Naturally I am interested in these men met, women met, so-called notable men and women with many of whom I have formed friendships. But—this fact may disappoint you who have happened to pick up this book—these notable ones are not and have not been my central interest. Some of them may appear in the pages of my book and others may not; and if they do appear it will be but incidentally—for, in my writing, I have always written of "obscure" people. It is these who have given me life.

There is still another desire. I would like to write a book of the life of the mind and of the imagination. Facts elude me. I cannot remember dates. When I deal in facts, at once I begin to lie. I can't help it. I am by nature a story teller. No one ever taught me. Like such men as Erskine Caldwell, Ring Lardner and others I've known, I'm a natural.

Once, many years ago, I sat down to write the story of my own boyhood in a Middle-Western town. I couldn't do it.

When, for example, I wrote of my own father and mother I depicted people my brothers and my sister could not recognize.

"Anyway," I said to myself, "I have made a picture of my father and mother--" They were my father and mother as I felt them.

I remember once, a good many years ago, going on a fishing trip with several men friends. Marco Morrow, later Senator Arthur Capper's right hand man out in Topeka, Kansas, publisher of Arthur's *Topeka Capitol* and a lot of farm papers, was of the party, and Frank Dunn, then publisher of the *Chicago Post*, was along. There were half a dozen of us, all except myself newspaper men and we were staying at a fishing lodge somewhere far up in Minnesota.

The point is that the proprietor of the lodge was a man who took my fancy. He was one of the sort of men I am always making up stories about. Such stories become very real to me. All sorts of odd absurd things happened at the table up there in the fishing lodge.

Well, our host had a certain quality. Everything he said had to me a certain delightful naivete. I began to invent speeches for him.

And then later one night in Chicago at a dinner table I began to report some of the man's absurd and amusing remarks. I was going good. I had the whole table laughing at some of the remarks made by that man of the Minnesota lakes and woods when a man at the end of the table caught my eye.

It was Marco Morrow and there was a look of astonishment in his eyes.

I was just about to launch forth on a new anecdote when he spoke.

"Ladies and gentlemen," he said, "we have here with us this evening the champion liar of the world. He has been telling you stories of happenings in a fishing lodge up in Minnesota. He has been using me as a stooge for some of his stories. He forgot that I was here, listening. You see I was also one of this party of which he has been speaking. Not one of all these happenings with which he has been amusing you really happened."

Marco rose in his place at the table and bowed to me.

"Go ahead, you liar," he said. "Don't let me stop you. Don't let the truth get in your way." Just the same and although Marco did rather take the wind out of my sails that evening (I had forgotten that he was one of the party and I had convinced myself that all the stories I was telling that evening were true)--just the same, I swear that, although I may have been inventing some, I had really got the quality of our host at the fishing camp. If he had not said some of the things I made him say he should have said them.

What I am here trying to do comes to the same thing. I believe in the imagination, its importance. To me there is a certain music to all good prose writing. There is tone and color in words as in notes in music.

Persons also have a certain tone, a certain color. What care I for the person's age, the color of his hair, the length of his legs? When writing of another being I have always found it best to do so in accordance with my feeling. Besides, men do not exist in facts. They exist in dreams. My readers, therefore, those who go along with me, will have to be patient. I am an imaginative man.

Besides, I shall tell the tale as though you, my readers, were personal friends. We are walking together, let's say on a country road. The road follows a stream and the day is pleasant. We are unhurried. We stop at times to sit on rocks beside the stream. We arise and walk again and I talk.

I keep talking, love to talk. I am telling you that this thing happened to me, that that thing happened.

Do you wish I would stop talking, let you talk? Why then, dear readers, go write your own books.

--from *Sherwood Anderson's Memoirs*, "This Book"

The commercial aspect of thing(s) is really more deeply seated in all of us than we quite dare allow ourselves to realize. I constantly myself have men come to me, men who I think love me too, and say: "Now, Anderson, you could write a novel or a play that would make money. Why don't you do it and thus make money enough to be a free man? Afterward you could of course do your real work."

One is, you see, to make a mess on the very floor of the temple wherein he worships.

--Letter to Trigant Burrow, October 12, 1921, from *Letters of Sherwood Anderson*, #61

....*Marching Men* didn't come off, and didn't sell. Thereupon I gave John Lane, who was no doubt rather discouraged with me, the little book of verse called *Mid-American Chants*. How many copies of that little book were sold I do not know. But if I learned it sold two hundred I would be surprised.

It cooked me with that house all right. So when I offered their American representative *Winesburg, Ohio*, he turned it down. There had come the moment which comes to any man who is a writer. It is a moment a good deal after all like another one in every young man's life. I refer to the moment when, perhaps after a long campaign—let us say that we are referring to a young man in a village, when for weeks he has been courting—and she has been, time and again, on the point of surrender and then, at last, the moment comes—he has got her. It is a little like that, the moment when, to the man who has been struggling with words, courting them, they at last begin to march.

You are sitting at your desk. Oh, how many hours you have sat there! What stories, novels, songs, begun! Some of them have even been finished, after a fashion.

But you are dissatisfied.

"No. That is not it. I have not yet found it."

You have been getting too many ideas from the work of other men, from books read. We all begin in that way. A man has, in this way, gone to school to George Borrow, to Balzac, to Flaubert, to Turgenev, to George Moore, all of whom I, for example, had been reading assiduously.

"No. That is not it. Chuck it."

There is this life, in the streets through which you walk daily, life in men in shops and factories where you have worked. You were a boy in an American small town. You ran about the streets there. You worked for a time as a delivery boy for a grocer. You were for a time a newsboy, you delivered papers, went to kitchen doors. Because you were a seller of newspapers you, unlike other boys, could go into saloons. You saw men getting drunk, heard their talk. There would be these thousands of impressions in your mind. The journalist in doing his daily job must, at once, on the spot, use these impressions, but with the imaginative writer it is somewhat different. He must wait. He is like a woman who has become pregnant. Often I have found that an impression got for a story must stay in me for years. It comes into my mind, stays for a time.

Perhaps I try to write it but it is not there. I must throw it aside. (I think for example of a story called *Death in the Woods*. It is a story I must have tried to write at least a dozen times over as many years. I am not one who can peck away at a story. It writes itself, as though it used me merely as a medium, or it is n.g.)

I had been published. Books, with my name on their backs standing on a shelf over my desk. And yet, something eating at me.

"No. I have not yet written." These words whispered to myself in the night.

"It is not my own clear reaction to life. I have been following paths made by other men. I must find my own path."

--from *Sherwood Anderson's Memoirs*, "Book IV, The Literary Life, 1. Waiting for Ben Huebsch"

This book has become my confessional. Formerly I tried in another book—unpublished—to make what I call a Testament.

I tried to do it in song but the song broke.

The making of a testament, or rather a confession, is a kind of relief.

When I go into a church I find myself unable to kneel before a priest or a preacher. As the need of a symbol has been strong in me I have tried other things. I have been in turn a river worshiper, a moon and sun worshiper, a mountain worshiper. Often I have followed a child through the streets.

Once when I had been drunk and had been with a so-called fallen woman I did something that nearly led to my arrest.

Nearly all physically strong men have periods of pure flesh worship. I had been in such a period and had picked up a woman in the streets.

She did not understand my mood. Why should she understand? This was in Chicago. We went into a house and I stayed there all night. I tried to talk with her, to tell her something of my young man's impulses, of the confusion in me that had led me to her but she could not understand. She had been cheated, buffeted, beaten.

All prostitutes are morons. The clever, alive prostitute of fiction does not exist in fact. Writers are prone to be sentimental about prostitution because they spend so much of their own lives walking close to the line of their own kind of prostitution.

When I had been with the woman all night I left in the early morning. The sun was shining brightly. In the streets children were playing.

That day I got drunk and in the afternoon went into a park. Seeing a child with its mother I followed.

At last I ran to the child and falling on my knees tried to apologize.

It was not understood. People thought me insane. Kneeling before the child I muttered a few words about life, the sources of life and how they were befouled.

The mother, being frightened, screamed—the child stared at me.

I escaped through bushes and running a long way got into a street car.

   •   •   •   •   •   •   •   •   •

I had to laugh at myself and you will laugh.

It doesn't bother me—not now.

At last after seeking many confessionals I came to paper. I am humble before these sheets. They are clean.

I write my testament upon them. It is all I can do.

--from *Sherwood Anderson's Notebook*, "Notes Out of a Man's Life"

Again I have come from a writers' conference. I was there with several other professional writers. We lectured. We read manuscripts. After reading the manuscript of a novel, or of several short stories submitted, it was part of our job to take the young writer aside, have a talk with him or her.

That, we all found, was the hardest part of it all.

I think we were all eager to hand out words of praise and encouragement. We professional writers went from one to another.

"Have you read Miss Smith's manuscript?

"Well?"

There was the hope that the other had found something you had not found.

Among ourselves we talked big.

"Ah, tell her to quit writing. It's hopeless. Tell her to chuck it."

It is so easy to talk big when you are not in the actual presence of the young writer.

But wait. They are not all so young. There are men and women of forty and even fifty who have been at it for years. How patiently they have struggled. Evidently there is something corked up in such a one that needs uncorking. Life has hedged him about.

There is a woman who has made, let's say, a bad marriage but she is one who does not believe in divorce. She is grimly determined to stick it out, but something within her keeps wanting to run away.

Or a man is hedged about by a family. He is, we'll say, a clerk who has all his life, dreamed of a life of adventure.

They are both trying to get through words what they cannot or dare not try to get in life.

How can you help being sympathetic? It is something we all do. All of us no doubt spend a large part of our lives living in impossible dreams.

So there you are, in the presence of such a one. What are you to say? The manuscript you have been reading was bad enough. People in the novel or story were pushed ruthlessly about. They were made to fit into a crudely conceived plot.

But there is the writer sitting with you. I am quite sure that almost always such a beginner knows in his heart, or wherever a person does know such things, that his manuscript is bad, but he has this queer belief that a word from you will make it good.

So he sits with the expectant, hopeful light in his eyes.

And what are you to do, what are you to say? To say what you are really feeling would be like striking a child with your fist.

"Ah, go on home. Be a good wife, or a good husband. Go join the army. Get a job in a sawmill."

You can't do it. You hedge. In spite of yourself, when you see no hope, you begin saying hopeful words.

"Keep at it," you say. "Write more and more.

"The way to learn to write is to write."

You get off these old sayings. Let us say that there were, in a long novel you have waded through painfully enough, a few passages.

There was a description of an evening's walk, by a tree-lined road, just as darkness was coming on. At least that was felt. It was a little oasis in the desert of words. You cling to that, praise it, make much of it. You make too much of it.

And all the time there are the eyes looking at you. They are accusing you.

"You could tell me if you would," the eyes are saying. There is this belief that you have, concealed somewhere in your pocket, a key that, if you would but pass it out, would open all doors.

It is all very discouraging, very sad, except that now and then when you have grown most indignant with yourself, something sometimes happens.

"Why have I let myself be put into this position?"

It isn't only at writers' conferences that these things happen to you. Young writers come to your house, bringing manuscripts, or they send them by mail.

You grow furious.

"What right have they?"

You flee from them. You take it out on your wife. You are like a fish, hooked, that cannot escape.

And then—now and then—at long intervals—the thing happens. You remember a day, long ago, when you picked up and read a story by a man you knew, a Bill Faulkner or an Ernest Hemingway.

And, even at writers' conferences, it sometimes happens.

You have picked up another manuscript, feeling the hopelessness of it all, swearing to yourself that you will never again let yourself be persuaded to come to such a place, and there before you, on the white sheets, it is.

People in the story or the novel you hold in your hand become a little alive, really moving through the story, something really felt, a little actually put down.

It seems to justify it all, all your past embarrassment, your annoyance and anger.

There is someone really doing it. Again the sun warms you, the rain wets you. There is no gladness like the gladness that comes with the finding of another real writer just beginning to really throw the ink.

--from *Sherwood Anderson's Memoirs*, "Book VI, Life, Not Death—7. After a Conference"

Dear Lucile Cox: I'm glad you told me of the outcome of the trip to California and am more glad than I can tell you for your understanding of the difficulty of Ivor's present situation.

Of course I knew, from the few minutes talk I had with him, that his outlook on writing was utterly corrupt, but he can't be blamed for that. The man has probably never had life and its purposes dignified by putting it in any other terms than money and success.

What he is is probably something like this: a young man who has in him the making of an artist and at the same time a man who doesn't even know what an artist is. He came into my office and talked of writing a book as though it were a matter like going out and getting an advertising contract. Ye gods! Does he think there are no men who haven't minds and hearts above such cheapness? I wish he could know personally, as I have, some of these men who are the big selling successes and get big prices for stories in the *Saturday Evening Post*. I'd like him to know what cheap, vain, slick, oily men they are with their second-rate successes.

Can't you get the man to read a few things? Get him to read, if you can, Waldo Frank's *Our America* and Van Wyck Brooks' *Letters and Leadership* and *America's Coming of Age*.

One thing is sure. If he has in him the making of an artist, the fact that this California trip has fallen through is the best thing in the world. He might have written some second-class bunk about Chinese gods or something of that kind and had a cheap newspaper success. Then he never would have had a chance to see the light.

What I hope now is that he will realize that anything worth-while has to be come at by long, patient effort. He doesn't need to worry. There are plenty of cheap, flashy men. The fact that he hasn't ground out another second-rate book won't hurt. The world will lose nothing.

Of course, all America is losing tremendously all the time, because there isn't anyone to tell these young men, who might possibly be artists, that they are on the wrong road, that they should learn some humbleness and most of all learn to face themselves.

It will be interesting now to watch this man. Will he go to work to educate himself, to find out what the few real artists in America are talking about, and let writing go until he has found out a little about life;

or will he flop back into business and try to find there the quick, cheap, flashy success a man can get by making a lot of money by some form of trickiness—in other words, is the artist in him big enough and strong enough to begin standing on its own feet one of these days?

--Letter to Lucile Cox, (at one time a secretary of Anderson's), December 13, 1921, from *Letters of Sherwood Anderson*, #68

Chapter Six

Inspiration

What kept Anderson writing?

Dear Brother: I am drunk with the inclination to write. Such times come to me. I have to keep away from people, because every person I see is a big story. I have written a story called "The Net"* that is a marvel. It is one of the best things I have done.

You are wrong about the songs. Your argument that I will make more progress by bringing out the novels is all right, but don't you see that I must snap my finger at the world? That must remain a part of my creed. If a road leads to destruction, one must take it as a sporting proposition.

Every day I think of you with the Draft hanging over your head and you trying to get on with the book. Take it quiet and easy if you can. Go for a walk and look at people. Remember that in the vast hordes we are just minute figures. Nothing matters but the long swing of things.

The songs will perhaps not be printed. I have not heard from Jeff Jones** and have a hunch he has lost his nerve. Love to Margaret

(The following is apparently a long postscript.)

There are certain days when one seems to have the strength of some gigantic and prehistoric monster. It has been so with me today. I worked for hours and then went to walk in the smoky street. A storm swept over the city. Against the black sky the hard snow, half hail, was driven furiously. The people hurried shivering along. I wanted to embrace them all, men and women. It seemed to me that within my old shell was room for them all, that there a fire burned at which they could all warm themselves.

All day my mind has reached out and out. I have thought of everyone and everything. Minute little happenings in the lives of many people have been revealed to me. Today, had I a dozen hands, I could write a dozen tales, strange, wonderful tales, all at one time.

One wears himself away at such times. I did not try to work, but walked and walk(ed). A storm swept in from the lake, and the rolling, tumbling waters answered something in me and quieted me. Such times cannot last, but they are glorious. They are the reward of holding firm against the daily, dreary commonplaceness of everyday life. When they come, it is revealed again how truly and really life is worth while.

--Letter to Waldo Frank, after October 29, 1917, from *Letters of Sherwood Anderson*, #19

* Not published.

** Jefferson Jones, New York manager of the John Lane Company, the English publishing house which had brought out both *Windy McPherson's Son* and *Marching Men* in New York and London.

...With the publication of *Winesburg* I felt I had really begun to write out of the repressed, muddled life about me. The book, followed by *Poor White* and last year by *The Triumph,* (which) you have, gave me artistic recognition in America, France, England, and Germany. The books are now being translated into French and German.

However, they have had no popular success and have brought me little or no money, but that doesn't matter too greatly. One eats and sleeps and is no longer engaged in buying and selling. Life goes more happily. The recognition I have had from the world of artists here and in Europe is also sweet.

--Letter to Peter Ochremenko, January, 1923, from *Letters of Sherwood Anderson,* # 73

...Also I've had too much prominence. It isn't any good. It's bunk.

A man's one happiness is in his craft, for me the white sheets on which to write words that may have a tang to them and color to them.

--Letter to Jerome Blum, ?February, 1923, from *Letters of Sherwood Anderson*, # 74

I've been in Greenville, the big textile center, for three weeks and now am at Augusta.

Of course, as you will have guessed, I'm feeling around.

I suppose I am looking for the swing, the music, that will set me off. I guess you know I've been pounded a good deal lately by the smart young men, but I can't write my kind of prose without poetic content.

Lately I've been feeling for it in machinery, the inside of modern factories. I told you I was on the labor thing, but that is misleading.

I've had this idea for a long time, that the most exciting thing in modern life is on the inside of factories, where writers so seldom go, the whirl and wonder of modern high-speed machinery and, of course, incidentally, what it is doing to people.

I've an idea I had a kind of sneaking notion I would write a modern love novel and get money to go on with this.

I wrote the novel and then couldn't stomach it.

So I've pushed off into this vast river of modern machine energy, and although I have no money now and hardly know from month to month how I am going on, I do go on.

I wrote one long thing, (which) I sent to Otto, I call "Labor and Sinclair Lewis." He is trying to place it for me, but do get him to let you read it before you go.

I think it has got dance and reality in it.

Incidentally, I'd like your lady to see it. I've a notion it would get her.

Anyway there is something on the inside of factories no one has touched in prose.

It's the biggest thing I've ever tackled and some days shakes me to pieces.

I'm going to stay in the big cotton, silk, and rayon mills another week, go down to New Orleans to rest for 10 days, and then to Birmingham to tackle the inside of steel mills.

--Letter to Horace Liveright, ? late February, 1930, from *Letters of Sherwood Anderson*, # 172

...Just now I am terribly interested in factories and am spending a lot of time in them, looking at them inside, talking to factory owners, workers, etc...

I wish I could explain to you and Morrow* what I am up to. I guess you know that I have been one of the outstanding little protesters against the machine age.

However, it is here, and recently I have had a change of heart. I have been trying recently to go to machinery as a man might go to the mountains and to the forests and rivers. I have always had an idea that writers spend too much time in little groups and in cities. That is one reason that I, after being many years a city man, went back to the small towns...

The factories are really marvelous places. You know how you feel when you go into a press room. I am after that feeling in prose...

God, man, if I could get you and Morrow into the loom room of a big cotton mill at night. Why, it is a Niagara Falls of steel, of dancing lights, of power...

--Letter to Nelson Antrim Crawford**, February 20, 1930, from *Letters of Sherwood Anderson*, # 171

*Marco Morrow.
**Nelson Antrim Crawford, editor of the *Household Magazine*, Topeka, Kansas, on February 11, 1930, wrote Anderson asking for "a little article on small-town life."

Dear John: "Sunday morning and raining." I had just written the above sentence, intending to write you a long letter, when I put the sheet aside and began writing on my book. I have perhaps written 2(,000) or 3,000 words since then. Now I am tired, and my hands are shaky. It is still raining, harder than ever. I shall have to take a drink of moon to write to you at all.

What I want to say is something about the delight that may finally come to you in such moments of work. You may come to get out of canvases what I get out of sheets of paper.

I presume it is the power of losing self. Self is the grand disease. It is what we are all trying to lose.

I think the reason I want you to be an artist, have an artist's viewpoint, is just because such times compensate for so much else.

How people ever lose themselves who are not artists I do not know. Perhaps they, some of them do it in love.

> --Letter to John Anderson, ? April, 1927, from *Letters of Sherwood Anderson*, # 141

All this desire of revelation I found among the new acquaintances in the little converted retail storeroom at Fifty-seventh and Stoney Island Avenue in Chicago—Floyd Dell, Arthur Davidson Ficke, Lawrence Langner, a patent lawyer interested in the theater, coming now and then from New York to give us a feast with drinks, to speak to us of the new figures, Eugene O'Neill, Jigg Cook and others coming to the front in the East, Ben Hecht, Alexander Kaun, occasional young professors from the University, talk and more talk.

A kind of healthy new frankness in the talk between men and women, at least an admission that we were all at times torn and harried by the same lusts.

Our own lusts faced a little. It meant everything to me. And then excursions on the week end to the country, often to the lake country, the dunes south of Chicago.

Ben Hecht, having just read Flaubert, walking up and down declaiming. Ben then, as he remained, full of strange oaths, adjectives falling over adjectives, Mike Carr with his little red beard and light red bathing trunks flirting with every woman he met, "it is my purpose to be sincerely insincere," and reciting Swinburne by the hour. Alexander Kaun, telling again his tales of life in Russian villages, myself, hearing more and more of Russian writers, Tolstoy, Dostoievsky, Chekhov, Turgenev, a new world of writers to be opened up to me later.

Was I not later to be called, by one of our American critics, "The Phallic Chekhov"?

I am trying to give here an impression of what was to me a gay happy time, the gayest and happiest I have ever known, a feeling of brotherhood and sisterhood with men and women whose interests were my own. As yet I had not begun to face what every practitioner of any art must face, the terrible times of bitter dissatisfaction with the work done, often the difficulty of making a living at your chosen work, the facing of the petty jealousies that pop up among fellow craftsmen, the temptation, always present, to try to get into the big money by attempting to give them what you think they want, the times when the ink will not flow, when you have worked, perhaps for weeks and months, on some project only to have to face the fact on some sad morning that it is all no good, that what you have attempted hasn't come off and must be thrown away.

All of this still ahead of me during that summer with my newly found fellows.

And then the women. How we do need them. There were two Marjories, Margy Currie, who had been Floyd Dell's wife, and Marjory Jones, a very attractive black-haired woman of twenty-five, and a photographer. It is to such women that a man takes his first work.

"Now you tell me frankly what you think."

To be sure a man doesn't mean that. What he wants is praise, to be reassured, and it is this that women understand.

For often enough for the young worker it is only praise that helps. "Yes. You have real talent. Do not be afraid."

Such a woman will often remember for years some sentence you have written, and how it sirs and flatters a man to have such a sentence remembered and repeated. It is a special gift some women have, due perhaps to a lack of the competitive feeling in them, they wanting to make you happy and being not too scrupulous about it, thank Heaven for that.

So there was that summer, to be always remembered, the days got through in the advertising place and then the summer evenings, the walks in the Park, the gatherings in one of the little rooms. Arthur Davidson Ficke, already itching to throw all of that over and to devote himself to poetry, coming to town to give us a blowout. Wine, whiskey, and beer brought in. Some singing. Ben Hecht trying out a play in a tiny theater arranged in one of the rooms.

The week ends at some little town on the lake shore, six or eight of us men and women sleeping perhaps, or at least trying to sleep, under one blanket by a low fire built on the shore of the lake, even perhaps going off in the darkness to some secluded spot to bathe, all of us in the nude, it all quite innocent enough, but such a wonderful feeling in us of leading a new, free, bold life, defying what seemed to us the terrible stodgy life out of which we had all come. And then perhaps a walk during the evening alone with one of the women. For me it would have been with little Margy Currie, her hand on my arm.

I would have given her an attempt at a story to read.

"Do not be afraid, Sherwood. You have real talent.

"You will do it. You will do it."

--from *Sherwood Anderson's Memoirs*, "Book III, A Robin's Egg Renaissance, 5. Margy Currie"

I go about, when I am well and strong, with eyes and ears open. So much pride of life in these queer creatures and in myself.

They fascinate me.

Then the other reaction.

My daughter Mimi, Miss Eleanor Copenhaver, and I drove to the state fair at Richmond.

We lived in an upper-middle-class hotel there.

There I saw dead faces about me. There is something about prosperity, the hunger for it, the pretense in all these middle-class Americans, that makes the soul sick.

I presume that is why I keep going back to the workers, poor people with little pretense to them.

They give me, often when they are unaware, honest reactions.

Human nature peeping out. It is like color to you.

You have, I should say, to watch out. You will get that upper-middle-class thing there. It mustn't sour you on people.

Go sometimes, Charles, when you are not working, on solitary walks. If you can do it, stop and talk to Negroes, poor farmers, etc. We, as artists, ought to keep that human love alive in us if we can.

We have to fight for it, I guess, like any love...

Anyone hurt or twisted by life, to find the wonder in them.

I don't forget that one of the clear, lovely little water colors you did had a shithouse in it.

--Letter to Charles Bockler, September 21, 1930, from *Letters of Sherwood Anderson*, # 182

It was winter in Chicago and I wanted the South. There was the dreary round of advertisements to write, day after day.

"I will have to quit this. I am using here the words that are the tools of my real trade. I am soiling my tools."

Having saved a little money I went to Mobile, in Alabama. I had never been there. I had just put my finger on the map.

Perhaps I remembered how Grant, after he had taken Vicksburg, kept wanting to go to Mobile.

They wouldn't let him. They called him East to meet Lee, made him the head of all the armies.

But there was no danger of anyone's making me head of anything. I was glad of that.

I was in Mobile, on a winter day, had found a room in an old house, not far from the bay. It was a rooming house in which dock workers lived.

It was night and I went to walk. It was one of my memorable nights.

I thought the city very beautiful. It had begun to rain, a soft slow rain and I walked through a little park, in the heart of the city. Something happened to me.

I had come out of the park, where, even on the winter night, there was a scent of flowers and had got into a dirty, poorly lighted street when my foot struck something on the pavement.

It was a pocketbook and I picked it up. It was filled with bills. I hurried back to my room.

There was a billfold and in it was a hundred and forty dollars.

What luck. I sat in my room counting the money over and over. I do not think it occurred to me that night that the money belonged to someone else. It seemed sent to me by God.

A hundred and forty dollars. Why, it meant two or even three months more of freedom. There was a novel I wanted to write, the novel I did begin and carry along all that winter.

It was the novel *Poor White*. I wanted to tell the story of a town, what happened to it when the factories came, how life in the town changed, old patterns of life broken up, how the lives of the people of the town were all affected by the coming of the factories. The book has since become a sort of historic criticism of that change. It is used nowadays by a good many historians to give present-day students a sense of the so-called industrial revolution brought down into a single American town.

197

I was in the Southern city and had suddenly grown rich. Although I did look in the newspapers for the next several days I never saw any demand for the return of the money. I wondered what I would do if there came any such a demand.

I went again out of my room, into the rain of night, having hidden the money in my room. I walked. I was so excited I couldn't sleep. I was free. Now, for weeks, perhaps for several months I would not have to write advertisements. I had got into a Negro section of the city. It was late, after midnight, and the streets in which I walked were unpaved. There were long rows of little shacks and although it was so late I could hear voices in the houses. There was something found, a new adventure for me. It was in the voices I heard in the night, in the dark muddy little streets. There was something, not tense, not full of the false excitement and nerve-tension of the advertising place and, for that matter, of all Chicago. I heard soft voices. I heard laughter. There was a Negro woman's voice, perhaps speaking to her man.

"Now, honey, you be quiet. We got to sleep now."

It wasn't what the woman in the house said. It was the timbre of her voice, something I felt that night in the Negro street, something I wanted. It seemed to break something in me.

There was that money found in the street and hidden now in my room. There was the soft black southern night, the gentle rain, the voices of Negroes in the darkness, something in me released. I had been thinking—"Now I have these few free weeks and months. I must work hard, constantly. If I am ever to do this novel, I so want to do, I must be at it at once. I must work on it day and night."

The feeling of tenseness was still in me, the rushing, pushing Chicago streets still in me, Illinois Central trains to be caught, to be at the office at just a certain hour, a time clock to be rung.

Or, when I had moved to the North Side and came down into the Chicago Loop afoot in the morning, no time to lean over the rails of the old wooden bridges then spanning the Chicago River, to watch the gulls floating so beautifully over the lathery, green water of the river.

Freedom. Soft voices. Laughter.

"Be quiet, honey. We got to sleep now."

I found myself, on that night, my first night of freedom in the far South, going along in the Negro streets saying over and over the words of the Negro woman to her lover.

"Be quiet now.

"No hurry.

"Let your book come as it will."

A great sense of relief, of tension taken off, something I have always got in the South. It made me very happy that night. I must have walked for hours in the rain. I talked to myself, reassuring myself, an old fear that had long been growing in me, that I would never succeed in escaping the advertising place, that I would never get to the work I wanted, quite gone.

"Why I could sleep here in the street. A few cents a day would buy me food here."

Earlier in my walking that night I had gone down to the docks and there was a banana boat being unloaded. Ripe bananas were lying about and I had picked up and eaten two or three.

"I could feed thus, as a bird or a beast feeds."

It was all absurd enough, I dare say, the feeling of the Southern night, the Negro voices gave me, but it was all wonderful to me and I remember that later, as I walked in the rain that night, I doubled my fist into a hard knot.

"The North, from which I have come, is like this," I said, speaking along to myself.

"And the South, I have found, like this."

I opened my fist, let it lie open and relaxed before me.

--from *Sherwood Anderson's Memoirs*, "Book III, A Robin's Egg Renaissance, 10. The Conquering Male"

...it gives me some essence of new dignity in myself to get this letter that tells me that you, in spite of your difficulties, poverty, humiliations (I know you have had to face) are upright and working. It makes the air sweeter I breathe.

--Letter to Charles Bockler, (Late 1933), from
Letters of Sherwood Anderson, # 241

...I have begun working again and yesterday, for the 1st time in months, sat at my desk, here in this little country hotel, for hours with no consciousness of time passing, completely lost, the words and sentences with a fine rhy(th) mic flow, ideas coming like flights of birds, for the time, at least, completely happy.

No. Happiness is not the word. To be happy there must be consciousness of self as happy, and in this state there is no self.

I remember the first time this feeling ever came to me. I was living in a rooming house in Chicago. Already I had written and published a novel. It came, I think, from reading other men's novels.

It may have been that I was born to be a writer. I had perhaps read a lot of novels. "I can do that," I said to myself, and did.

But on this day I had come home from the place where I was employed very tired. My room was small and cheerless enough. I was discouraged and blue, hating the work by which I made a living.

I sat there at my desk and suddenly picked up my pen. I think every man must be filled with a thousand impressions, feelings, impulses that never get expressed.

Suddenly I began to write as I had never written. It did not seem to be me sitting there holding the pen. There was no me. It was as though some mysterious force outside myself had taken possession of me.

There were people everywhere, thousands, millions of people wanting their stories told. They didn't want it glossed over, made glamorous. That, in the end, only hurt and made life more difficult.

"If you knew my story, you might like, even love me a little."

That seemed to be the cry.

It was as though one of these began to speak through me. The pen began to run over the paper. I did not seek for words. They were there. They seemed to leap out from my hand to the paper.

Now there was no such thing as time, no little shabby room, no rainy street outside the window. Life was there on the sheets of paper, word(s) marching, sentences marching.

I don't know how long I sat that day. When my tale was finished, I got up and stood. Tears came. I cried because I was happy. I had written something that was solid and true. There was no fakiness, no false glamour. There was a beauty that perhaps few people would find or understand. I think I must have felt as a woman feels after a birth, when she has her first babe in her arms. I kept saying words to myself. "It's there. It's solid. It will stand there like a rock. If no one else knows, I know."

I was both proud and humble. It was almost as though God had reached a hand down out of the sky and touched me.

It was again a little like that yesterday. It doesn't come often. There are long times of waiting. I tell you all of this to explain why a man can't go to Hollywood.

Anyway such moments, when they do come, are worth all of the waiting.

--Letter to Charles H. Funk,* Late May, 1935,
from *Letters of Sherwood Anderson,* # 263

*Charles H. Funk, lawyer in Marion (Va.--author) and one of Anderson's closest friends there. The two men corresponded frequently during the '30's. Andy is Funk's nickname.

It is dear of you to want me to have the things of your(s), and I want to have them. I get them out every day and look at them, and they are symbols to me of you and the real morality of you. They are living things to me, and I suppose that is what every artist wants—to leave thus living traces of the fine thing in himself for other craftsmen to see and understand a little.

--Letter to Alfred Stieglitz, June 30, 1923, from
Letters of Sherwood Anderson, #79

...I do not remember which of my stories I wrote that evening but I remember a young girl sitting on the porch of a house across a roadway.

She also was wondering what I was up to. She kept looking across at me. When I raised my eyes from the paper on which I wrote so rapidly, she smiled at me. The girl...she couldn't have been more than sixteen...was something of a flirt. She had on a soiled yellow dress. She had thick red hair. In such moments as I am here trying to describe the eyes see more clearly. They see everything. The ears hear every little sound. The very smell of the roots, of seeds and grass buried down under the earth, seem to come up into your nostrils.

The girl sitting on the porch of the house across the road from the railroad station, had heavy sleepy blue eyes. She was full of sensuality. "She would be a pushover," I thought. "If I were not writing this story I could walk over to her.

"Come," I could say to her. "What woman could resist such a man as I am now, at this moment?"

I am trying to give, in this broken way, an impression of a man, a writer in one of the rich moments of his life. I am trying to sing in these words, put down here the more glorious moments in a writer's life.

My mind moves on to other such moments. I was in a big business office, surrounded by many people. Clerks and other fellow workers in the office where I was employed walked up and down past my desk.

They stopped to speak to me. They gave me orders, discussed with me the work in which I was engaged, or rather the work in which I was presumed to be engaged.

I had been for days in a blue funk. I had been drinking. "Here I am condemned day after day to write advertising. I am sick of it." I had been filled with self-pity. No one would buy the stories I wrote. "I will have to spend all of my life in some such place as this. I am a man of talent and they will not let me practice the art I love." I had begun hating the men and women about me, my fellow employees. I hated my work. I had been on a drunk. For several days I stayed half drunk.

I sat at my desk in the crowded busy place and wrote the story, "I'm a Fool." It is a very beautiful story. Can it be possible that I am right, that the thoughts I now am having, looking back upon the two or three hours when I wrote this story in that crowded busy place, have any foundation in fact? It seems to me, looking back, on that particular morning as I sat at my desk in a long room where there were many other desks, that a curious hush fell over the place, that the men and women engaged in the writing of advertisements in the room, advertisements of patent medicines, of toilet soaps, of farm tractors, that they all suddenly began to speak with lowered voices, that men passing in and out of the room walked more softly. There was a man who came to my desk to speak to me about some work I was to do, a series of advertisements to be written, but he did not speak.

He stood before me a moment. He began speaking. He stopped. He went silently away.

Do I just imagine all of this? Is it but a fairy tale I am telling myself? The moments, the hours in a writer's life of which I am here trying to speak, seem very real to me. I am, to be sure, speaking only of the writing of short stories. The writing of the long story, the novel, is another matter. I had intended when I began to write to speak of the great gulf that separates the two arts, but I have been carried away by this remembering of the glorious times in the life of the writer of short tales.

There was the day, in New York City, when I was walking in a street and the passion came upon me. I have spoken of how long it sometimes takes to really write a story. You have the theme, you try and try but it does not come off.

And then, one day, at some unexpected moment it comes clearly and sweetly. It is in your brain,
in your arms, your legs, your whole body.

I was in a street in New York City and, as it happened, was near the apartment of a friend.

The friend was Stark Young and I rang his bell.

It was in the early morning and he was going out.

"May I sit in your place?"

I tried to explain to him. "I have had a seizure." I tried to tell him something of my story.

"There is this tale, Stark, that I have for years been trying to write. At the moment it seems quite clear in my mind. I want to write. Give me paper and ink and go away."

He did go away. He seemed to understand. "Here is paper. And here is a bottle."

He must have left me with a bottle of whiskey for I remember that as I wrote that day, hour after hour, sitting by a window, very conscious of everything going on in the street below, of a little cigar store on a corner, men going on in or coming out, feeling all the time that, were I not at the moment engaged with a particular story I could write a story of any man or woman who went along the city street, feeling half a god who knew all, felt all, saw all...I remember that, as I wrote hour after hour in Mr. Young's apartment, when my hand began to tremble from weariness, I drank from the bottle.

It was a long short story. It was a story I called "The Man's Story." For three, four, five years I had been trying to write it. I wrote until the bottle before me was empty. The drink had no effect upon me until I had finished the story.

That was in the late afternoon and I staggered to a bed. When I had finished the story, I went and threw myself on the bed. There were sheets of my story thrown about the room. Fortunately I had numbered the pages. There were sheets under the bed, in the bedroom into which I went, blown there by a wind from the open window by which I had been sitting. There were sheets in Mr. Young's kitchen.

I am trying as I have said to give an impression of moments that give glory into the life of the writer. What nonsense to mourn that we do not grow rich, get fame. Do we not have these moments, these hours? It is time something is said of such times. I have long been wanting to write of these moments, of these visits a writer sometimes makes into the land of the Now.

On the particular occasion here spoken of I was on the bed in Stark Young's apartment when in the late afternoon he came home.

He had brought a friend with him and the two men stood beside the bed on which I lay. It may have been that I was pale. Stark may have thought that I was ill. He began pulling at my coat. He aroused me.

"What has happened?" he asked.

"I have just written a beautiful, a significant story and now I am drunk," I replied.

As it happens I have not re-read the story for years. But I have a kind of faith that something of the half mystic wonder of my day in that apartment still lingers in it.

--from *Sherwood Anderson's Memoirs*, "Book IV, The Literary Life, 8. Writing Stories"

Now, Brooks, you know a man cannot be a pessimist who lives near a brook or a cornfield. When the brook chatters or at night when the moon comes up and the wind plays in the corn, a man hears the whispering of the gods.

--Letter to Van Wyck Brooks, early April, 1918,
from *Letters of Sherwood Anderson*, # 29

Chapter Seven

The Writer as Self

Is there a difference between a writer and him or her self as a person?

I awake. I am depressed. My nerves have gone back on me. I sleep in the room where I work, liking to be near books, my desk, the smell of ink.

When I awake I know I cannot work but I arise hopefully. There is a pile of white sheets that I have covered so that dust does not settle on them.

Now I brush the cloth of my desk, rearrange my books and papers.

I shall not write today. My nerves are on edge. I am incapable of sustained thought or feeling. I think perhaps I am getting old, that my capacity for sustained work is gone forever. The thought sends a shudder through my frame. I shall walk about today seeing strong well men everywhere. I want to kill some man, take from him his youth and strength and go gayly on my way. Well I have had a little of that. He may have mine. Let's trade.

I want only strength to sit here at my desk all day. I want the words and sentences to march across the sheets. Let someone else sign all I do. If any fame is to come to me let someone else have it.

I want to work. It is my life. I want to gather together the thousand impressions of life that have come to me.

I want to put meaning and music into prose.

But I shall not be able to work today. My nerves are shattered.

I must go out, flee from this desk, go walk in the streets.

I put on my clothes and go away. I feel like weeping when the day comes wherein I cannot work.

--from *Sherwood Anderson's Notebook*, "Notes Out Of A Man's Life, Note 12"

Try to remain humble. Smartness kills everything.

The object of art is not to make salable pictures. It is to save yourself.

Any cleanness I have in my own life is due to my feeling for words.

The fools who write articles about me think that one morning I suddenly decided to write and began to produce masterpieces.

There is no special trick about writing or painting either. I wrote constantly for 15 years before I produced anything with any solidity to it.

For days, weeks, and months now I can't do it.

You saw me in Paris this winter. I was in a dead, blank time. You have to live through such times all your life.

The thing, of course, is to make yourself alive. Most people remain all of their lives in a stupor.

The point of being an artist is that you may live.

Such things as you suggested in your letter the other day. I said, "Don't do what you would be ashamed to tell me about."

I was wrong.

You can't depend on me. Don't do what you would be ashamed of before a sheet of white paper or a canvas...

You won't arrive. It is an endless search.

--Letter to John Anderson, ? April, 1927, from *Letters of Sherwood Anderson*, #140

I believe he (i.e., Mark Twain—author) wrote that book (i.e., *Huck Finn*—author) in a little hut on a hill on his farm. It poured out of him. I fancy that at night he came down from his hill stepping like a king, a splendid playboy playing with rivers and men, riding on the Mississippi, on the broad river that is the great artery flowing out of the heart of the land.

Well, Brooks, I'm alone in a boat on that stream sometimes. The rhythm and swing of it is in some of my songs that are to be published next month. It sometimes gets into some of the Winesburg things. I'll ride it some more, perhaps. It depends on whether or not I can avoid taking myself serious (ly). Whom the gods wish to destroy they first make drunk with the notion of being a writer.

--Letter to Van Wyck Brooks, early April, 1918, from *Letters of Sherwood Anderson*, #29

...I had been faking for so long a time both as a manufacturer and as an advertising writer, working so long with my tongue in my cheek, that I had begun to fear that everything in my nature was poisoned by fakiness. True, I had tried to make a philosophy for myself. I had clung to the idea that I could preserve an honest mind. "I am not responsible for the society into which I have been born," I had told myself. It might be necessary to be a pretender. But you must not lie to yourself. At moments I had had visions of a life I might lead. There was the real world in which I was immersed, and there was this other world, the world of fancy. I had come to think that it also could have a reality. People could exist also in it. I had felt my struggle in the lives of many of the old writers. I presumed it had also existed in the lives of the painters. I had talked over the matter with my brother. But if in the world of my physical existence I had become a slick one, at bottom a crook, would this not affect my life in the world of fancy? I asked my brother this question. "There are these figures in the world of the book, the story. They are constantly being sold out." At that time as now, our magazines were filled with so-called plot stories. A kind of violence was being done in the imaginative world. People were being sold out there, and the plot story to my mind was the result of the domination of the writers by business, which was ruling more and more in America—the result of the influences which made slickness and trickery inevitably a part of business. "To sell out a character in a story is the same thing as selling out your friend or your lover in life," I told my brother.

But wasn't my own work as a writer being touched by the same slickness? (I think all of my earlier work was. Like most young writers I had copied many of the tricks of successful American writers.) In seeking to divide my life I was fighting a losing battle. How indeed could I spend my days often being clever, being an actor, doing work in which I did not believe, and then come home and make a straight and honest approach to this other work? How could I be half a crook and half a straight and honest individual? "A man's life shows up in himself," I thought. "My novel may have impressed them but they will immediately be on to me myself." So I hid myself that evening in the bushes.

But there was a movement in the room and presently all emerged into the street. They crossed the street, seeming to me a gloriously happy group, and went into the Park. They were going to walk by the lake. For a time I followed, muttering to myself, "I will never be a part of such a group. How can I? What am I but an advertising writer?" Afterward, when I got to know him, Floyd Dell once hurt me bitterly by saying to me the very words I was saying to myself that night. We had got into a quarrel. "You are only an advertising man who would like to be an artist," he said.

--from *Sherwood Anderson's Memoirs*, "Book III, A Robin's Egg Renaissance, 5. Margy Currie"

...The central notion is that one's fanciful life is of as much significance as one's real flesh-and-blood life and that one cannot tell where the one cuts off and the other begins. This thing I have thought has as much physical existence as the stupid physical act I yesterday did. In fact, so strongly has the purely fanciful lived in me that I cannot tell after a time which of my acts had physical reality and which did not. It makes me in one sense a great liar, but, as I said in the *Testament,* "It is only by lying to the limit one can come at truth."

--Letter to Alfred Stieglitz, June 30, 1923, from *Letters of Sherwood Anderson,* #79

Dear John: I think you must do very well if you do no more than to give yourself to the mood of the moment like that. I have so often made a fool of myself and suffered for it afterward. I have gone somewhere in a certain mood and, in the effort to come out of it and join with the others, have gone too far. Evenings when I have talked too much, drunk too much. I have been partially in love with ladies and in the enthusiasm of the moment have led them to think I was ten times as hard hit as I actually was.

You have to pay dearly for being an imaginative person. You see a great deal and feel a great deal, but there is ugliness to see and feel as well as beauty, and in yourself as well as in the others.

I fancy what you have to try to learn is to give as little time as possible to self-pity. That seems to spoil most imaginative men. They are a bit more sensitive than others. They exaggerate the consequences.

As you well know, this is the real reason why the arts may be of help. It is ten times as important to be devoted as it is to succeed. You will be a fool if you think ever that you have succeeded in the arts.

Actually I would take in as many phases of life as I could. Give yourself all you can now to the people about. Let yourself enter into these moods. You have always the danger of letting yourself grow too introspective. Knowing all you can know of the surface of life will not hurt you.

(P.S.) Lots of love.

--Letter to John Anderson, ? March, 1929, from *Letters of Sherwood Anderson*, #157

A little success. There you are. Some money comes in. I have had two years of comparative leisure and look back upon them aghast. "My God, what have I done with them?" The question frightens me.

When I was at work at something other than writing, I had at least the feeling that I was doing something out of necessity. Earning your living gives a certain sense of virtue. It is even good to feel wronged a bit. You know how it is.

And so here am I. No, the book is not done. I do not know when it will be done. I have thrown it aside.

Well, I have come to a resolution. I shall go to work at something other than writing. As you know, formerly I was in the position you are in. I made my living, not by teaching, but by advertising writing. My other writing was incidental. I had not tried to make a slave out of my pen. It could play over the paper.

Then corruption crept in. "Give me leisure," I cried, "and you will see what I shall do." The gods laughed. I got the leisure.

Long days nothing to do. "Write, man." But what shall I write?

I am sitting on a hill in the country or walking in the streets of a town. I am in despair, such despair as you know.

Well, I argue with myself. "But, man, you do not have to write. Live."

But I have come to live by writing. I want beauty and meaning always at my finger tips, and there is no beauty or meaning anywhere in me.

But I am only reviewing a state we are both often in. It is not new to you.

What I sat down to do was merely to give you news of myself. I have got a home now in the country. It is almost paid for. The country is very lovely. It does not cost much to live here.

Well, I am going to a nearby town and go to work. I am at present in negotiation for the purchase of a small town weekly paper.* If I secure it, and I hope I shall, I will become a country editor. The paper can make me a living. I shall live by it and not by scribbling.

All of this to get something of my own weight off the back of my pen in order that, if the gods are good, it may run a bit more lightly over the paper.

*In Marion, Virginia

218

Really, and what a curse to be an artist at all. It is the only way of life. It is at the same time the most terrible way of life. Sweet Jesus, Holy Mary, mother of God, why did you not make me a bricklayer, or a plumber?

I can imagine crawling under houses to fix drains. I look up through a crack in the floor. I see the slender legs of the woman of the house, wish to possess her. My days pass so. I get drunk and go home and beat my wife. On the whole a comparatively good life. At least when I lay my hands to a pipe, I can fix the pipe. You see what I mean. What offended me in your letter of the spring was, as you know, that you addressed me as a kind of great man, one removed from the things that sometimes almost drive you insane. I would not be so removed. O(h) my dear man, work accomplished means so little. It is in the past. What we all want is the glorious and living present.

--Letter to Roger Sergel, ? October, 1927, from *Letters of Sherwood Anderson*, #147

...I know the road I took long ago, but when I try to think of talking to anyone with any notion that what is good for me will be good for them, I draw back.

Primarily the difficulty with all of us is that, being Americans, we in some way got a wrong start in life. The notion of success in affairs, in love, in our daily life is so ingrained that it is almost impossible to shake it off.

You perhaps do not know that I was married and the father of three children, that I had to undertake the delicate and difficult task of breaking up that marriage* and of trying to win the real love of that woman out of marriage and outside the difficulties and complications of sex.

For myself I found it necessary to disregard all of the smart conclusions of the men of my time and set up gods. I found it necessary to my continued existence to utterly and finally embrace failure, the one terrible, hard thing for an American to do.

That was the year, Frank, that I went into the Ozark Mountains. I took the woman and the children with me. I lived in a separate cabin on a hillside, and together the woman and I went through poverty, hatred of each other, and all the terrible things that can come from such a situation.

It is odd now to think that it was misunderstanding that brought us through. She came to the conclusion that I was not mentally sound. That awoke the mother instinct in her. We began to make progress.

No story I will ever write will touch that story, and that is one of the keenest pleasures of life to me, that I lived something beyond any power of mine to write of it.

--Letter to Waldo Frank, ? March, 1917, from *Letters of Sherwood Anderson*, #7

*Sherwood and Cornelia Lane Anderson were married in May, 1904, and divorced in the summer of 1916. His three children—Robert, John, and Marion ("Mimi")--were by this first marriage.

Naturally your interest in my craft touches me deeply. I am so made, Ferdinand, that I should have gone insane long since but for this devotion. For it I have sacrificed a lot, life with my own children, perhaps in the end the respect of that great body of people, simple and good, much of my work has offended.

It goes deep, the whole impact of such an attitude as I have taken, into the structure of a man's life. To such a man as myself, who can only grow in expression, some of the expression is bound to miss fire.

One learns so slowly. Will the true balance come in the end? Perhaps not. What I may always be hungering for is the perfect artist who cannot exist...

I feel, and more so now than ever, like one just coming to the foot of the hill one is to try to climb. I think it was that very reticent Joseph Conrad—who, I am afraid, would have little use for me, but for whom I have much use—who said that the writer only lived after he began writing*, and by that method of reckoning I am but 10 years old.

--Letter to Ferdinand Schevill, ? December, 1923, from
Letters of Sherwood Anderson, #92

*See Conrad's *A Personal Record*, Harper and Brothers, 1912, p. 174: "...A writer is no older than his first published book..."

One thing I have found out. I cannot continue to live the life I have lived as a businessman. In a sense I have been like one living in a damp, dark cellar ever since I went back into business after my few months of freedom in New York last year. To think straight at all I had to get temporarily out of it. In New York I did.

Several things happened. I saw the O'Keeffe things and the Stieglitz* things. I went into a gallery and saw some paintings of Renoir. I found out again the old lesson that one cannot muddy oneself and be clean.

I shall have to get out of business at once, within a month perhaps. I know nothing of how it can be done. I only know it must be done. If it cannot be done, I shall get out anyway and suffer what loss of friendship and what ugly hatred is necessary. Children like mine do not come of a breed that starves.

--Letter to Waldo Frank, ? December, 1919, from *Letters of Sherwood Anderson*, #43

*Georgia O'Keeffe (1887-), painter, and Alfred Stieglitz (1864-1946), photographer. They were married in 1924. The famous "Little Galleries of the Photo Secession" in New York, generally known as "291," were devoted to exhibitions of advanced and modern work.

I do not believe I can write of my own marriages, being fair to both myself and the women involved. Once I was speaking of them to a friend.

"What is the matter with me, Frank?"

"Such fellows as you are often strong-headed," he said. "The demands you make of life are, you know, rather terrific. Most men finally accept the harness that life puts on them. You fellows cannot. You would die if you did.

"I'll say this for you," he added. "You do take life seriously. You believe in it. Many men come to the place where they take women purely as physical facts. Intimate contact with them is a physical necessity but it is that and nothing more.

"Fellows like yourself demand more. You keep demanding this strange thing we call love. When it dies out you go. You spend your life searching for it."

My first three marriages each lasted exactly five years. I have always been sure that none of the women were to blame when our marriage failed. Any practitioner of the arts is a trial to live with.

We are never there. We go away, often for months at a time.

Well, we are there physically. We are in a house, or in a street, but we are at the same time far away.

One of us is, for example, writing a novel. For months he will be off away from the people immediately about. Inside himself he is living another life, often having nothing to do with the people with whom he is living his own physical life. Speak to him and he will answer you, but he does not really hear. You make an engagement with him. You are to meet him on a certain day, at a certain hour, in a restaurant or at a theater. Do you think he will keep it? Very likely he will not. When you made the engagement with him your words did not register on his mind. He heard but did not hear.

It was because he was not there. When you spoke to him he seemed to be sitting at his desk in a room in the house where you lived with him but in reality he was in the captain's cabin of a ship, far out in the Pacific.

There was something tense going on in the cabin of the boat. There were two men and a woman in the little room. There had been a storm and the ship, a small one, had been disabled. It was drifting.

The captain of the ship, an old man, had a young wife and the mate wanted her and she had fallen in love with the mate. It was the ancient story.

The two men and the woman are having it out, there in the cabin. You see, the ship is leaking and will soon go down. It is a question of taking to boats, the boats perhaps drifting far apart.

Is the woman to go in the boat commanded by the captain or in that commanded by the mate, the man she loves? It may well be that, before they leave the cabin where they now sit facing each other, one of the two men will have been killed.

See how the woman standing there by the door trembles, how white she is.

So...as the writer is watching all this, a fourth unseen figure in the little ship's cabin, his own wife, comes to him. She wants to make an engagement. There is something she wants him to do for her.

"Sure. All right. Certainly I will."

Why, he did not hear her at all. Her words were blown away by a wind. They did not register on his mind.

Who was that who came into this room? My wife? What is a wife? I have no wife. Did I marry someone? Where? When?

It is dreadful to live with such a man. It is only possible...Only a saint could do it.

There are months and months when you are merely dust under his feet. For him you have no existence. As well, during such times, be married to one of the dummies in a store window.

Almost all of my own friends, men of the theater, painters, musicians, have, in this matter of marriage, had the same experience I had had. They have tried and failed, tried and failed. Some of them, upon the break-up of a marriage, have grown bitter. They write novels making the women the central character. They grow bitter and ugly about it all.

How absurd. When one of us makes a failure of marriage it is, almost inevitably, his own fault. He is what he is. He should not blame the woman.

The modern woman will not be kicked aside so. She wants children, she wants a certain security, for herself and for her children, but we fellows do not understand the impulse toward security. When we are secure we are dead. There is nothing secure in our world out there and, as for the matter of children, we are always having children of our own.

For example, someone is always asking me which one of my own stories I like best, and I have a pat answer for them.

"Go ask some mother who has had several children which one of them she likes best," I answer.

It is a changing, shifting world, this world of the imagination in which we who work in any of the arts must live so much of our lives. We have it and then we have it not. Oh, the blank days, the black despair that sometimes descends upon us.

We grow irritable. Speak to one of us at such a time and you will probably get a sharp nasty answer. Trust us and we may betray your trust.

No. Do not ask me to write of the women with whom I have lived in marriage. I respect them too much to do it. That I have found a woman who, after ten years with me, can still laugh at me, who understands my wrinkles, who is there beside me, smilingly willing to forgive my idiosyncrasies, who after seeing through the years we have lived together my worst and my best—that is my good fortune.

I am one of the lucky ones. Good luck has always been with me.

I dedicate this autobiography to my wife, Eleanor.

--from *Sherwood Anderson's Memoirs*, "Book V, Into The Thirties, 1. A Dedication and an Explanation"

Dear Mr. Copenhaver: I am writing you this little note for two reasons. For weeks and months I have wanted to talk with you, but I have found it very hard. You are not an easy man for me to talk to, and I feel perhaps a lot that you do about the risks Eleanor is taking in marrying me.

Also I am a writer rather than a talker and, I think, can say better what I feel in writing.

As regards Eleanor and myself. We have known each other a long time now. We began as friends and then began to love each other. She has done some wonderful things for me. When I first knew her and we were but friends, I was almost altogether a defeated man.

She gave me new courage, made me see myself, I believe made me a workman again.

As men our two lives have been, I should say, altogether different. I have taken great risks, made mistakes you haven't made. In my own way, I think, Mr. Copenhaver, I have also been a God-seeker. To be the kind of writer I have been and am I had to take risks of misunderstanding. I thought that to understand men and women, get at the inner secret of them, was more important than to gloss over life.

I have been punished for that, misunderstood often. It is, I believe, partly, maybe altogether, the secret of my failure in marriage. I have got in some places the reputation of being what I am not, a sensual man. I do not believe my life would show any such thing.

On the other hand, Mr. Copenhaver, I have got, by the course I have taken, the love and loyalty, I believe, of some of the finest men in America. On the whole I can't apologize. In the end I will stand on my work, and it is because Eleanor has had a real sense of that always, has helped me so much, has stood by me when I was discouraged and defeated that I love her so much, more than I ever thought I could love.

Mr. Copenhaver, I am sorry and hurt that the occasion of our marriage should not be a time of joy and gladness. I wish with all my heart I had found Eleanor earlier. I didn't. I would like to be friends. Even yet, if you can convince her, or if she has any waverings, I will release her from any promise to me.

I am sorry to have been the cause of worry and anxiety to you. Sincerely

--Letter to B.E. Copenhaver, Eleanor's father, ? June, 1933, from *Letters of Sherwood Anderson*, #235

I think that in myself, Charles, I am prejudiced against the rich. Perhaps I do not feel that they are any worse than the poor, but that they have too great a handicap. It is so difficult, if you are made to stand out a bit from the mass, not to assure yourself that it is all due to some special virtue in yourself. All power of money or place therefore brings a kind of corruption almost inevitably. The poor and the obscure escape, not because of some special merit, but because their chances are better.

This feeling has grown in me. Sometimes I do think that I am foolish in this. I am no longer young and have made no provisions for the future. Sickness or misfortune might well assail me. Still I do not want to make any provision at all for the future. Now I rather live from day to day, a little money always drifting in, enough to keep me afloat. Suppose in ten years it stops.

I used to look with horror, for example, upon the fate of Melville. There were years of his life when he was an old man, as I will presently be, and when he had nothing. He had to live a strange life of obscurity in a little hole, as did also the painter Albert Ryder.

Why, it does not seem anymore such a sad fate. I should be able to gather up remembrances on which I can feed. I think of that often in the night.

For example, women. There were hours with Mary, for example, that are shining things. They stay fresh in my mind. They belong to me as surely as any other kind of profession.

--Letter to Charles Bockler, February 10, 1931, from *Letters of Sherwood Anderson*, # 195

...Sometimes when I go like a beggar asking warmth, comfort and love from another, knowing I do not deserve it, I begin living a little in others, and thus I get away from self.

As for the end, I have often thought that when it comes, there will be a kind of real comfort in the fact that self will go then. There is some kind of universal thing we will pass into that will in any event give us escape from this disease of self.

I believe, Burt, that it is this universal thing, scattered about in many people, a fragment of it here, a fragment there, this thing we call love that we have to keep on trying to tap. I know that I am being vague in speaking of this, because it is likely that no one of us will ever find it in all its fullness and richness in any one other person, and I know also that I am trying to express the inexpressible.

You know, Burt, how I have always hit at money and positions. The whole subject isn't as important to me as you may think, and the only reason I hit at it is because I think it often gets in the way of understanding. I can't help half wishing that you and I were two penniless tramps, with a loaf of bread between us, sitting perhaps on a railroad embankment and waiting for a train. The only thing about money or the lack of it is that it gets into our thoughts when it shouldn't. If we were the tramps spoken of, perhaps it would be a little easier for each one of us to comprehend the difficulties in the nature of the other.

You see, Burt, I am not saying exactly what I want to say. I want to say that in spite of everything life is a grand show. I don't think we can ever quit. I know that sometimes I myself have had to try and be like a small child learning to walk again. I have walked along streets, saying over and over, to myself, "Now I must look, watch, and listen." I was trying to say to myself that if I could grasp the details of a building, the beauty of a woman's figure, the trouble in another man's eyes, this painting, the street, the stretch of fields and hills--

Why, Burt, do we need to feel that we must always do? Children are not like that. They are very often happy in just being, and I think we have to grasp at that and keep trying and trying, over and over, just to be and always to flee away from self and into others.

Now, Burt, I do not believe that any contribution I can bring amounts to much, but I do believe that I have sincere affection for you, and the fact that I have is also proof that the same kind of affection is coming toward you from many people.

This is the real inner glory of life, Burt, and I believe that all we can do is to try to keep realizing that this thing does exist in others and to try all the time to feed upon it and to go toward it to escape self. Sincerely

--Letter to Burton Emmett, May 8, 1933, from *Letters of Sherwood Anderson*, #233

I very much don't want to be a public figure. In America it just happens to do something very strange to a man. Let yourself be taken up, made a public figure, and they do something terrible to you. I've seen so much of it.

I've been told sometimes that my writing has had a pretty deep effect on other and younger writers in the country. A good many of the better young writers have told me so. That's better. You throw a stone in the pool, and the circles spread far out.

Not that I've ever had any idea of being an influence. I like best to think that I'm just a storyteller and a pretty good liver. To me it's like this: there are people everywhere you go. They talk. The voices go on endlessly.

But they are not saying what they think, what they feel. Very well. If you can keep something quiet and a little relaxed in yourself, you can, sometimes, hear the unspoken words people are saying. That's better. It seems to get you a little way along.

For people are very lonely, terribly so.

I used to think I wanted to change everything, smash it. I don't now. I guess I really began writing because I wanted to get off self and found that, sometimes, I could by absorbing myself in others.

--Letter to Margaret Bartlett, ? November, 1939, from *Letters of Sherwood Anderson*, #387

Dear Morrow*: To date it seems to us the most satisfactory thing we have done.**

Please note that absolutely natural editorial "we." I got rather sick of the professional air my position as writer was taking on. It is too much like being a professional lover. It can't be done.

And if I did not want to be in the position of making my living as a writer, what else was I to do? There was the matter of going back into an agency as a copy man. I hate backtracking like that. A big steamship company offered to send me around the world. I'm sick of running around the world. And it only meant hack writing for them.

Or hack writing for some magazine or publisher. This chance came up. I took it. Here I am. I am sending you an issue.

I rather hope the "What Say?" column may amount to something. People here like it. It might catch on as a thing that could be syndicated and make some dough for me that way.

Many times I think of our talks in the old days. We both wanted to be writers. I got there. You didn't. To tell you the truth, old man, I can't see much difference. I think my next novel will be about that—the man who succeeds and what comes of it.

There is always the chance, and a strong chance, of the separation (from) life of the professional writer. A man becomes famous. I suppose I may say I have done that.

It only means you become a public character, and who wants that? I hold to the opinion that writing should be an incidental part of life, not the leading thing in life. If you acquire fame, people begin putting you outside themselves. You are something special. Who wants to be that?

In a sense this whole thing is a sinking of myself back into life. It is a great sea, this thing we call life, and I like swimming in the sea. I have been in the desert too long.

Oho for the open sea of country journalism...

--Letter to Marco Morrow, December, 1927, from *Letters of Sherwood Anderson*, #148

*Marco Morrow and Anderson had become friends during 1898 when they were living in the same boardinghouse in Springfield.
**At Morrow's request Anderson was sending him a copy of one of the two Marion newspapers, probably of the *Smyth County News*.

Now I am getting up in the morning at six and am at my desk at eight. I do everything. A man wants a little handbill got up for the sale of steers. I write it for him. An old mossback farmer comes in and spends an hour trying to get me to knock off 25 cents on the subscription price of his paper. I enjoy it all and in the moments I catch am writing again. That is what a man lives for.

--Letter to Alfred Stieglitz and Georgia O'Keeffe, December 19, 1927, from *Letters of Sherwood Anderson*, #149

One lives so much in an imaginative world, imagined people, crude often enough, but with tender realities in them too; then one is shocked, hurt by the immaturity, the bad-boyishness of men. Why will they not let themselves see the beauty in things about, in one's own work sometimes, too? Each man is afraid of his neighbor, outdoes him in vulgarity to seem manly.

--Letter to Alfred Stieglitz and Georgia O'Keeffe, December 7, 1923, from *Letters of Sherwood Anderson*, #91

...At my best I am like a great mother bird flying over this broad Mississippi Valley, seeing its towns and its broad fields and peoples and brooding over some vague dream of a song arising, of gods coming here to dwell with my people. At my worst I am a petty writer not big enough for the task I have set myself.

It is needless to say how much your letters have meant to me. Like yourself I cannot understand the competitive spirit among writers. We are all so inadequate in the face of the thing to be done; life among us is so brief and so hurried that to pause and snarl at each other is unspeakably dull.

Well, you don't do it, and thank God for you. Your brotherly affection and understanding is the biggest thing I've struck since I became known as a writer. For that alone it was worth while publishing. My love to you

--Letter to Waldo Frank, before November 18, 1917, from *Letters of Sherwood Anderson*, #23

It is of course blithering folly for any of us who are aiming to have any fun out of writing to expect recognition or give a damn about it. What does it amount to anyway? Perhaps silly women mouthing over you. The real writer who got recognition in the country now would be like a bush pissed on by a long procession of dogs. I have my own way of getting recognition. I recognize myself. I have got me a lot of gaudy little feathers, red and green and purple, and I wear them in my hat. That is like putting your finger to your nose in the midst of a desolate place.

I have a chance to go to New York, but think I will stick to my stinking town. I am in a way part and parcel of the muddle out here. The stink of the stockyards is in my clothes.

Brother, I can only think of one thing to beg of you. Keep a swagger. Spit in the eye of the greasy world. Do be of good cheer. The winds and rains come, and the land is black with fertility. Men will be born, infinite men of broad girth and cocky eyes. Escape if you can all the art and intellectual talk. Go wide and free like a good-gaited colt.

--Letter to Waldo Frank, After November 18, 1917, from *Letters of Sherwood Anderson, #24*

So I have been a writer now for thirty years and on too many days I still write badly. I have been panned and praised by critics, have been called a genius, a pioneer, a heavy-thinker, clear-headed, muddle-headed, a groper. That last has stuck more persistently than any of the others. If it is meant, by groping, that I do not know the answers, O.K. During most of my life, to date, I have been healthy and strong. I am no prize fighter, no athlete, but I enjoy thoroughly my friends, women, food, drink, sleep. There is a kind of persistent youth in some men and I am one of that sort. I rebound quickly from disaster, laugh a good deal, make rather quick and easy connections with others...

And I say that when I die I should like this inscription put on my grave...

LIFE, NOT DEATH, IS THE GREAT ADVENTURE.

--from *Sherwood Anderson's Memoirs*, "Book VI, Life, Not Death--, 11. The Fortunate One"

My life has been so rich and crowded that I want to tell something about it before the bell rings. It began just at the right hour and I hope it may not carry on too far. Physical life doesn't so much matter—the ability to win foot races, hit a baseball, ride a horse over jumps—but I would like to quit living just before that terrible time when the brain, the imagination, ceases from activity.

Still, whose life is this? What is your own life? I am one thing in my own consciousness, another as you see me, still another as I seem to Jane Grey or Tom Smith or John Emerson. Is there even such a thing as a life of one's own? Is it not some illusion, some limitation in ourselves that makes us feel there is? It seems to me that all lives merge.

--from *Sherwood Anderson's Memoirs*, "This Book"

Chapter Eight

The Writer in Society

How does a writer interact with those around him or her? Is there an obligation to the common good?

It may be now that a time has come to ask ourselves questions.

Are our lives worth living?

Is it living at all to spend all of our best years in helping to build cities larger, increase the number and size of our factories, build up individual fortunes, make more dirt and noise and indulge in an ever-increasingly louder talk of progress?

Or is there a quieter, more leisurely and altogether more charming way of life we might begin to live, here in America, instead of having to run off to Europe to find it?

Whether the time has come to ask the question or not, it is being asked. That is the most important question the younger generation is asking. A sharp and ever more and more searching criticism of all the old American shibboleths is going on. Books are being written and printed today that simply could not have found a publisher five or ten years ago and a new and vastly more intelligent audience has already been developed for these books. In the future—sometime perhaps—we will have less loud talk of freedom and more determined individual effort to find freedom for expression of lives.

--from *Sherwood Anderson's Notebook*, "Notes on Standardization"

Dear Brother: Your letter telling of things astir with you. I get the picture. You withdraw into a little close place, and the flame burns in you. When you are exhausted, you go forth and face life. It is dull, abjective, concerned with little things. Always the million empty voices shouting of nothing.

It is an odd thing how that shrillness got into America. My work takes me up and down the land a good deal. We have no forests out here, but there are tremendous open spaces with white farmhouses dim in the far distance.

Through Ohio, Indiana, Michigan, and Wisconsin were formerly forests. The men walked all day under great trees, followed by the women. They were cutting the timber away, making a place for our towns and cities.

For myself I can't see why we do not get more quiet into our lives out of just the contemplation of the things they did and from walking in the open places.

The mystery has to be solved. In some way we have got to come to an understanding of the cause of the shrillness and emptiness of our times.

Now, you see, here in the West there is an effort being made, but there is much silliness. We get here also young writers gathering in groups and chattering in a quite terrible way. On Michigan Avenue in Chicago young men and women strut along, striving to imitate the manner of the Parisian. They go into places and drink coffee and cocktails. They talk of art. They have notions, or seem to have, that they achieve something by a manner of walking or dressing. They get ahold of ideas regarding the shades of things. One of them to whom I talked actually spoke of "The Politics of Poetry." Do not be too much amused. The thing I am told exists and has its effect on the molding of opinion. It is infinitely silly, but it is a part of the shrillness of the times.

A curious notion comes often to me. Is it not likely that when the country was new and men were often alone in the fields and forests, they got a sense of bigness outside themselves that has now in some way been lost? I don't mean the conventional religious thing that is still prevalent and that is nowadays being retailed to the people by the most up-to-date commercial methods, but something else. The people, I fancy, had a savagery superior to our own. Mystery whispered in the grass, played in the branches of trees overhead, was caught up and blown across the horizon line in clouds of dust at evening on the prairies.

I am old enough to remember tales that strengthen my belief in a deep, semi-religious influence that was formerly at work among our people. The flavor of it hangs over the best work of Mark Twain. That's what makes it so moving and valuable. I can remember old fellows in my home town speaking feelingly of an evening spent on the big, empty plains. It has taken the shrillness out of them. They had learned the trick of quiet. It affected their whole lives. It made them significant.

One can say that the coming of industrialism has brought about the present-day emptiness and shrillness of the arts, and there must be something in the saying, but, Lord, man, can art be superseded by the clatter of the machinery in a shoe factory? The prairies are still here. The Mississippi flows southward to the sea. It is but a step from the heart of the Loop district of Chicago to the shores of Lake Michigan.

I suspect that the thing needed is quite simple—a real desire on the part of a few people to shake off the success disease, to really get over our American mania for "getting on." It has got to be pretty deep-seated if it gets us anywhere.

Why is the desire for success so deep-seated? I have wondered. Is it because we are neither urban or rural that we have neither the crude sincerity of the Russians or the finished gesture at art and life of the Frenchmen?

As for *Marching Men*, it doesn't matter. I know what I tried to do. In any event, if the thing I wanted is at all there, it will take time to grow and mature in the minds of others. That is what is happening to your book.* The sincere thing you put into it is beginning to be felt.

I'm grinning now. I take to myself a wide sense of leisure. I'm going to have my own way about the book on which I am at work if it never gets itself finished. We die and rot away, and the author of forty volumes would make no better fertilizer for the corn.

Don't let them crowd you, Brother. You don't have to do the job, and I don't have to do it. When we are dead, a million fools will survive us.

Every day that you work well is a good day. I know that, and I want good days for you, that's what I want.

--Letter to Waldo Frank, after November 7, 1917, from *Letters of Sherwood Anderson*, #22

The Unwelcome Man (1917).

As you no doubt know, I have been writing for a good many years and have had some success. On the whole, my success has been what I suppose I might call an artistic success, rather than financial. However, I have had no special reason to quarrel with my fate in that direction. either.

Until I was about twenty-five years old, I was a laborer and worked in factories. Later I went into business and was in business for about ten or fifteen years. For the last several years I have done nothing but write.

I have always tried to avoid the necessity of writing hurriedly for the popular magazine.

However, what you might call my fame has grown slowly. My last novel* sold very well indeed, and I have no doubt that if I were to produce another novel now, it would almost automatically sell well.

I did, indeed, write a novel last fall, which was on the theme of love between men and women, etc., and had even announced it for publication, but afterward destroyed it. This I did, because I felt it had been done rather hurriedly in order to get money to do something else in which I was now more interested.

I have been feeling for the last four or five years that the most interesting thing going on in American life is inside the factories, the growth of the machine, our new high-speed industrialism, its effect on civilization, etc.

I felt that most of us were writing about this and thinking about it from the outside.

I wanted to go to the factories, not only the cotton mills in the South, but to the steel mills, the automobile factories, and to many other such places.

I have already found out that what I am after is going to take a long time. I wanted to get the beauty and poetry of the machine, but at the same time its significance to labor. I have a feeling that the whole tendency of modern industry has been rather to dehumanize people. I felt that if I could go into the factories and stay long enough, I might begin to write, feeling as one of these people, my whole purpose being to give finally an expression, not about these people, but out of them.

Knowing it was going to be a long, slow job, I spoke to Miss Copenhaver about the possibility of having it financed, and she spoke to you.

*Dark Laughter, which in six months ending in December, 1925, sold 22, 603 copies.

Afterward I grew afraid. It seemed to me that there were so many places in modern life where money was more needed. Perhaps I shall come out all right without any help.

One of the things I wanted to do was to publish in the magazines that cannot pay so well. I would like to have the things I may do published in labor papers, many of which cannot pay anything.

As a sort of explanation of my occasional fright about finances, I might explain that I have three children. I went down into Virginia two years ago and bought two small weekly newspapers down there. My oldest son is now running these papers and is doing very well with them. I still owe $7,000.00 on the papers, although we are paying off some every year.

My second son is a young painter and, of course, will probably make no money for several years, and my daughter is still a schoolgirl. My oldest son and I plan to try and make the papers support him and the other two children so that I may be free to work at this job of mine in a more leisurely way and not feel hurried about it.

When I talked to Miss Copenhaver, I had in mind that someone might be interested in helping me get the papers cleared, but afterward I grew doubtful about it. It seems so foolish to ask for help in a thing such as I am undertaking, that may not after all turn out, and in a time when there are so many things on foot that need help.

I think, therefore, that I would be better to drop the whole matter for the time and let me see if I cannot fight it out alone.

--Letter to Miss Anne Bogue**, March 11, 1930, from *Letters of Sherwood Anderson*, #173

**Miss Bogue was apparently connected either with Mrs. Straight or with the *New Republic* group.

Something I had long wanted had come to me. I had got a book that was my own. I felt it was my first real reaction to life uninfluenced by reading. And what had I not put into the book! I thought it had my life, my feeling for life, my love of life in it.

Well, it was published. And immediately there was a strange reaction, a strange reception. In justice I ought to speak of the fact that criticism had been poured all over my Chicago contemporaries from the start. We had the notion that sex had something to do with people's lives, and it had barely been mentioned in American writing before our time. No one it seemed ever used a profane word. And bringing sex back to take what seemed to us its normal place in the picture of life, we were called sex-obsessed.

Still the reception of *Winesburg* amazed and confounded me. The book was widely condemned, called nasty and dirty by most of its critics. It was more than two years selling its first five thousand. The book had been so personal to me that, when the reviews began to appear and I found that, for the most part, it was being taken as the work of a perverted mind...in review after review it was called "a sewer" and the man who had written it taken as a strangely sex-obsessed man...a kind of sickness came over me, a sickness that lasted for months.

It is very strange to think, as I sit writing, that this book, now used in many of our colleges as a textbook of the short story, should have been so misinterpreted when published twenty years ago. I had felt peculiarly clean and healthy while I was at work on it.

"What can be the matter with me?" I began asking myself. It is true that nowadays I am constantly meeting men who tell me of the effect had upon them by the book when it first came into their hands and every now and then a man declares that, when the book was published he praised it, but if there was any such praise, at the time, it escaped my notice.

That the book did not sell did not at all bother me. The abuse did. There was the public abuse, condemnation, ugly words used and there was also, at once, a curious kind of private abuse.

My mail became filled with letters, many of them very strange. It went on and on for weeks and months. In many of the letters there were dirty words used. It was as though by these simple tales I had, as one might say, jerked open doors to many obscure and often twisted lives. They did not like it. They wrote me the letters and, often, in the letters there was a spewing forth of something like poison.

And for a time it poisoned me.

Item...A letter from a woman, the wife of an acquaintance. Her husband was a banker. I had once sat at her table and she wrote to tell me that, having sat next to me at the table and, having read my book, she felt that she could never, while she lived, be clean again.

Item...There was a man friend who was spending some weeks in a New England town. He was leaving the town one morning on an early train and, as he walked to the railroad station, he passed a small park.

In the park, in the early morning, there was a little group of people, two men, he said, and three women, and they were bending over a small bonfire. He said that his curiosity was aroused and that he approached.

"There were three copies of your book," he said. The little group of New Englanders, men and women...he thought they must all have been past fifty...he spoke of the thin sharp Calvin Coolidge faces... "they were the town library board."

They had bought the three copies of my book and were burning them. My friend who saw all of this, thought there must have been complaints made. He said he spoke to the group gathered in the little town square before the town library building...and that a woman of their group answered his question.

He said she made a sour mouth.

"Ugh!" she said. "The filthy things, the filthy things."

Item...A well-known woman writer of New Orleans. She spoke to a friend of mine who asked her if she had seen the book.

"I got fire tongs," she said. "I read one of the stories and, after that, I would not touch it with my hands. With the tongs I carried it down into the cellar. I put it in the furnace. I knew that I should feel unclean while it was in my house."

There are these remembered items and there were others, hundreds of others. Some of them were quite humorous. Winesburg of course was no particular town. It was a mythical town. It was people. I had got the characters of the book everywhere about me, in towns in which I had lived, in the army, in factories and offices. When I gave the book its title I had no idea there really was an Ohio town by that name. I even consulted a list of towns but it must have been a list giving only towns that were situated on railroads. And the people of the actual Winesburg protested. They declared the book immoral and that the actual inhabitants of the real Winesburg were a highly moral people. Once later, when the book began to make its way, the *Cleveland Plain Dealer*, as a Sunday newspaper stunt, sent a representative to the real Winesburg.

The reporter, a woman, wrote me about it. It must have been an amusing experience. She had interviewed a local preacher.

"Did you ever stand so, on a bitter cold night, in the belfry of your church, waiting to see a naked woman lying in her bed in a nearby house and smoking a cigarette?"

Perhaps she was not so bold. At any rate she wrote me that the people of the town declared that they had not read the book but that they had heard it was dreadfully immoral.

Later they softened a little. There was to be a town homecoming day and they wrote and asked me to come. A preacher living in the real Winesburg wrote and printed a little pamphlet on the town. He mentioned my book and the people of my book. He suggested that if I ever came to the real Winesburg I would find quite different people there. At least he must have read the book. The suggestion was that the people of the real town were not bothered by secret lusts, walked always in the straight line, lived what is called clean lives, and I remember that, when I read the little pamphlet, I was myself indignant.

For certainly the people of my book, who had lived their little fragments of lives in my imagination, were not specially immoral. They were just people, and when I answered the preacher's letter I told him that if the people of his real Winesburg were as all around decent as those of my imagined town then the real Winesburg might be indeed a very decent town to live in.

And here is something very curious. The book has become a kind of American classic, and has been said by many critics to have started a kind of revolution in American short-story writing. And the stories themselves which in 1919 were almost universally condemned as immoral, might today almost be published in the *Ladies Home Journal,* so innocent they seem.

--from *Sherwood Anderson's Memoirs,* "Book IV, The Literary Life, 2. I Write Too Much of Queer People"

It was in Chicago that I first knew other writers and men deeply interested in literature. I had come back to my big town to try again. I was living about in cheap rooming houses trying to get some ground under my feet, to give my own life some decent purpose and meaning, growing often discouraged and going off with others to carouse in so-called low saloons. And here in Chicago I wrote many of my best-known stories. It was in Chicago that the newspapers first both damned and praised my work...

Something was stirring at that time in the world of arts in America. I think everyone felt it. Little magazines with several of which I was to have connections broke out like measles in that period. There was the *Little Review* in Chicago. The *New Republic*, the *Seven Arts* and also what is now known as the *Old Masses* got under way in New York. In Chicago the old *Dial* changed hands—later on moving to New York. The impulse reached out over the country. There was a Mid-Western magazine called the *Midland*. In New Orleans another called the *Double Dealer*.

It was the time of the struggle for woman's suffrage, women parading, picketing the White House, going to jail. It was the time of the Little Theatre Movement, represented in Chicago by Maurice Browne. In writing there was what is now called "the Middle-Western movement." George Ade, the Chicago newspaper man, had attracted wide attention with his fables in slang. He had gone to New York, grown rich writing plays. Edgar Lee Masters, who had been a law partner of Clarence Darrow, was at work on his *Spoon River Anthology*. Carl Sandburg was at work on his Chicago poems. He was, I believe, a reporter on a socialist daily which afterwards failed, when he went on to the *Chicago News*. In the *Chicago Tribune*, Burt Leston Taylor was conducting his famous column and I believe Ring Lardner was writing baseball.

To Chicago from New York came the famous exhibit of modernist paintings known as the Armory Show. For the first time we saw the gorgeous work of Van Gogh, Gauguin, Cezanne and the rest of the French moderns. Thousands of citizens stood waiting at the door of the Art Institute in Chicago when the show opened. One of the paintings which roused a great clamor in the newspapers—it was called "Nude Descending a Staircase,"--one of the first of the abstract cubist paintings—was bought I believe by Mr. Sherwood Eddy.

It was a kind of outburst of energy and penetrated even to the copy department of the advertising agency where I was employed.

And how many remarkable men known, thoughtful friends made in those Chicago days. Henry Justin Smith, Ferdinand Schevill, Robert Morss Lovett, Burton Rascoe, Lloyd Lewis, Ben Hecht, Floyd Dell, Arthur Davidson Ficke, Harry Hansen, Carl Sandburg, Lewis Galantiere, Ernest Hemingway.

With these men and others I sat about in restaurants, talked of books, had the works of old writers brought to my attention, discussed new writers.

With Ben Hecht in particular I often went while he covered news stories. We quarreled and fought, made up, remained friends.

Other men not to become literary figures made lifelong friends. The big Irishman George Daugherty, one of the sweetest natures in any man I have ever known, and Marco Morrow, an ex-newspaper man and the closest thing to a genius I knew. Both were engaged in advertising writing. They were both from Springfield, Ohio, where for some six or seven months I had attended the Lutheran college known as Wittenberg, and I had known Morrow when I was in school there and for a time he and I had lived in the same house, a large boarding and rooming house filled with college professors, lawyers and writers, run by Mrs. Folger, of whom I shall have a charming story to tell. Then there was Roger Sergel, now at the head of the Dramatic Publishing Company. Talking with all these men of books and writers, drinking with them, sometimes spending most of the night walking and talking.

And then there was the fascinating figure, Margaret Anderson. I knew her when she burst forth with her *Little Review*, wrote for her first number, wrote for the old *Dial* when it was published in Chicago. I became a part of what was for a time called "The Chicago School" of writers.

How many men known, women known, during the years there. They come flocking into my mind, men of the advertising office where I was for long years employed as copy writer, men infinitely patient with me and my idiosyncrasies.

And there was that rather volcanic fellow, the Italian poet, Carnivali, who came from the East to help Harriet Monroe on *Poetry: a Magazine of Verse*. He sometimes raged about my rooms at night.

And Bodenheim, with his corncob pipe and the broken arm he carried in a sling, although it was but an imagined break.

It was the time of a kind of renaissance in the arts, in literature, a Robin's Egg Renaissance I have called it in my mind since. It had perhaps a pale blue tinge. It fell out of the nest. It may be that we should all have stayed in Chicago.

So many of us began there, got our early impressions of life there, made friends there. Had we stayed in the home nest, in Chicago, where it all began for so many of us, the Robin's Egg might have hatched.

There we would all have been chirping away and pecking at worms up and down Michigan Boulevard until this very day.

--from *Sherwood Anderson's Memoirs*, "Book III, A Robin's Egg Renaissance, 1. The Nest"

Dear Frieda Meredith Dietz: Your letter* is very interesting, but indeed it does arouse in me a desire to comment.

First of all, I think you are very courageous. I am a little sorry that you feel you must limit yourself to Southern writers. You see, I am not enthusiastic about the regional idea. I think any art expression, if it has any importance, becomes important only when it becomes also universal. You will pardon me. You see, I was born a Yank, of a Southern father to be sure, but in Yankee land. I got all my early impressions there, and while I love the South, I shall always feel rather an illegitimate son. It must, I think, have been instinct that led me, when I did settle in the South, to settle among mountain folk, who aren't, you know, very Southern. They are just people, and it is just people, not Yanks or Southerners as such, that interest me.

I remember once going to a dance of Southern cotton mill girls and boys in a cotton mill village in Georgia and, as I sat watching, amusing myself by picking out from among the dancers those who in some odd way suggested to my mind more or less famous people I had known. I assure you that I found there among the mill people a certain very aristocratic Southern woman poet whom I much admire. I found Theodore Dreiser, Harry Hansen**, John Marin, the painter. Please don't tell on me. I found James Branch Cabell. He danced just as Cabell would have danced had he been born a millhand.

So you see (how) hopeless I am about regional literature.

I shall turn your letter over to Eleanor, who will send you the data, etc., for which you ask. Can't you pay any money for articles, stories, etc.? I do so love money. Sincerely

--Letter to Frieda Meredith Dietz, after July 21, 1938, from *Letters of Sherwood Anderson*, #338

*On July 21, 1938, Miss Dietz wrote Anderson, saying that she and her brother, August Dietz, Jr., of The Dietz Press, Richmond, Virginia, were going to revive the *Southern Literary Messenger* and requesting support. It was to be "a revival of the 'Old South.'"
**Harry Hansen (1884-), literary editor of the *Chicago Daily News*, 1920-1926, and in 1938 on the *New York World-Telegram*.

...I remember that after such an evening we youngsters walked home rather quietly in the darkness. I boarded at the house of one Trundle, a teamster, and had to go the last three blocks alone. The man spent his days out of doors doing heavy work and except on Saturdays the house was early silent and dark.

Perhaps I romanticize this whole matter. I cannot quite make out. It seems to me now that, as I stumbled forward over uneven sidewalks in the darkness and sat afterward in the darkness on the Trundles' front porch looking at the blue-black summer sky and listening to the occasional night noises, the barking of a dog or the sharp sound of hoof beats on a distant road where some young farmhand was hurrying homeward after an evening in town with his girl; that at such moments something happened to me more deeply significant in my own life than any number of millions of tons of coal mined in a year, the profits and losses of coal mining companies, or the wage to be paid miners. For an hour I sat, and it seems to me that in that hour and by way of the old carpet-bagger something came floating down to me from many men of the old times who, on distant hills and in the streets of cities of an older world, had made songs that now were being resung within me. Sentences that, when the old man read them, had not issued clearly from among the march of many sentences now stepped forth and got themselves looked at and listened to. My lips reformed the sentences the lips of men now dead had formed and, perhaps, caught a little the rhythm, the swing, and the significance of them, and I am sure something of the same sort must have happened to the other lads who had spent the evening with me in the company of the old man. I was at that time intent upon learning the mysteries of the house-painters' trade and as I went through the streets on the next day clad in my overalls I perhaps met one of my companions of the evening before. We stopped and stood talking for a moment. Then he threw his arms above his head and began stretching and yawning. "I didn't get to sleep very early last night. After I went to bed I got to thinking and couldn't sleep at all," he said.

The whole point of which meandering tale being, I think, that it is entirely possible that we Americans may some day awaken to find we have long been traveling a blind trail toward fullness of life. It is true, isn't it, that what we want is leisure, a chance to live more fully? Does not the preamble to our Declaration of Independence say something about the pursuit of happiness?

For my own part the people I know and love all live in industrial towns and are all in some way slaves to that giant we have disturbed in his sleep under the ground, disturbed without really putting the harness upon him. I rather expect I shall myself live and die in such towns and I do not like the prospect, even though I may care greatly for the people who are in the same fix as myself. Things have moved with unbelievable rapidity in not only one but a thousand towns of Mid-America since I sat with my comrades on the porch of the carpet-bagger's house and heard from his lips the voices of poets. Within the year I have revisited that place.

On the particular street along which we looked on the summer evenings now stands a long row of factories, their grim walls reechoing at night to the footsteps of a new kind of men. It is quite true and must not be denied. The America of today is not the America of a very few years ago. As to the future America: can a youth spent at the movies, spent whirling through the streets in motor cars, or in the grim residence districts that almost inevitably grow up about factories in our towns or cities, be of the same quality as the youth of the last generation? Surely not. I do not deny to this newer youth its quality. Perhaps the only trouble with me is that there is something here I cannot digest. You see I'm only asking questions after all.

And there is one question keeps coming back and back, whenever my mind gets on this subject. It seems to me that love has much to do with the fiber and quality of men as citizens of a country and the whole matter of hustling pushing coal-mining factory-building modern life for the most part remains in my mind in the form of annoying and to me unanswerable questions. I find myself going about day after day and asking myself such questions as these: "Can a man love a coal mine or a coal-mining town, a factory, a real-estate boomer, the Twentieth Century Limited, a Ford, a movie or a movie actress, a modern daily newspaper, or a freight car? If a man live in a street in a modern industrial town can he love that street? If a man does not love the little patch of ground on which his own house may stand can he in any sense love the street, the city, the state, the country of which it is a part?" The questions are disquieting. The love of country is to my mind a necessary part of a full and happy life and I do not like to think that love of country may in the end be a thing like modern religion, occasionally pumped into temporary life by some political Billy Sunday and by propaganda in the newspapers.

Well, I write freely when I write what I feel and my own feeling is that coal and the industrial power that has come from coal and the coal mines is now king. The black giant, disturbed in his sleep, has set forth and has conquered. We all breathe his black breath.

Also I believe that self-respecting men, once they have accepted a town or a country as their town or country, do want to bring something like beauty into the place where their lives are to be lived and that in this king there is as yet little beauty. Having been disturbed in his bed in the hills he has set out, Hunlike, to conquer and will conquer. Even as I write he is on the march, with a vanguard of Rotary Club members, invading new towns, building newer and larger cities, breathing his black breath over greater and greater stretches of green country.

The king is, I admit, King.

What a laugh the word "democracy" must sometimes stir within his black bowels!

May one be ribald when a King is crowned? It has long been my desire to be a little worm in the fair apple of Progress.

As I sit writing and feeling very important and serious about this whole matter of what coal and industrialism is doing to the towns of the Middle West I do have to stop and for a sane moment think that I know little of the matter about which I have made all these words. And it happens I am at this moment sitting in one of the few spots in America where coal is not king.

Perched out on the lip of that Mississippi River that drains nearly the whole of Mid-America there is a city within a city. Where the new and modern city of New Orleans begins, some ten blocks away from where I sit, the king is King; but in this old French and Creole town, hidden away, half forgotten in its corner, we can make him sing low.

It is afternoon and cool here, and the night will be cooler. I shiver a little as I sit writing of that Coal King who is making so many great fires burn in so many places. I look at my empty fireplace.

From the street there comes a cry that is also a song. I run out on my little balcony and look down. A ragged negro is driving a bony horse along the street and to the horse is hitched a wagon with wobbly wheels. There are a dozen bushels of coal in the wagon and the driver has made himself a song.

"Do you want any coal?
It's gwy'an be cold.
Do you want any coal?
It's gwy'an be cold."

Is he one who sells three buckets of coal for four bits or does he give but two? There is a moment of intense mutual inspection and then from a window on the floor below my landlady comes to my rescue. She speaks sharply a few words of Creole French and a delightful grin spreads over the black face. "Sho, boss. Three heapen ones," he says, and comes up the stairway with my portion of fire and comfort in a broken bushel basket on his shoulder. He is preceded by my friend the landlady who has brought an old iron tub to sit beside my hearth and hold the coal.

And so all is well. I sit and contemplate mankind and such things as social progress or decay with a calm mind.

Why not? My fire burns! The King has been humbled.

The King is in a washtub and I burn his bones.

Another delightful thought comes. In the end the King may lose the battle, after all. It would be a delicious outcome of the whole affair if, gradually, year after year, an ever and ever increasing number of men should decide that the spoils offered in the King's service were not worth the price of service and should manage in some way to get the King at last into a place where he is compelled to coo him softly like a suckling dove, as he does here in this forgotten spot where Progress is unknown.

--from *Sherwood Anderson's Notebook*, "King Coal"

...In my room I sit thinking of courage—of the courage of men. The balls of the eyes of the boy on the track were numb and he could scarcely see. In the two rooms where he lived with his sisters there was a tiny coal stove by a window. It was put there to stop the cold from coming through the cracks in the window sill and that necessitated a long stovepipe having many joints. The pipe was fastened with wires and often at night it fell down scattering black coal soot on the bed where the boy lay. He could not eat when he came home but lay on the bed until his heart beat strong again and warmth came back into his body. At nine o'clock he arose, washed, had his supper, and returned again to sleep beneath the long stovepipe.

On my desk in my room there is a black leather note-book with leaves that may be taken out. When the leaves are all written full I take them out, fasten them with rubber bands, and put them away. Then I fill he book with new white leaves.

In my room when I come back from standing by the tracks I think how I was afraid because I had reached middle age. There is a cunning satisfaction in my heart because I think that when my body is weary I shall take the leaves from the rubber bands and go on publishing year after year as though I were yet alive.

There is satisfaction in this thought until another thought comes. Not as I stood weary by the tracks, but now, as I think of the hoarded leaves of white paper in the rubber bands, has the coward appeared. To myself I say, "Am I to be less stout-hearted than the boy who stumbled half frozen along the tracks?"

Are we, who write stories, who paint pictures and who act upon the stage to go on forever hoarding our minor triumphs like frugal merchants who keep a secret bank account, are we to be less courageous than our brothers, the laborers?

--from *Sherwood Anderson's Notebook*, "From Chicago"

Chapter Nine

The Beginning

How do we attain the title of "author"?

...if you intend to follow through as a writer, there is but one way.

To write and write and write, until presently the life in you and about you runs more and more naturally down through your hand to the paper.

More and more and more. I know no other way.

--Letter to John Paul Cullen, October 28, 1937, from *Letters of Sherwood Anderson*, #325

Books by Sherwood Anderson

Windy McPherson's Son, 1916

Marching Men, 1917

Mid-American Chants, 1918

Winesburg, Ohio, 1919

Poor White, 1921

The Triumph of the Egg, 1921

Many Marriages, 1923

Horses and Men, 1923

A Story Teller's Story, 1924

Dark Laughter, 1925

Tar--A Midwest Childhood, 1926

Sherwood Anderson's Notebook, 1926

A New Testament, 1927

Alice and the Lost Novel, 1929

Hello Towns, 1929

Nearer the Grass Roots, 1929

The American County Fair, 1930

Perhaps Women, 1931

Beyond Desire, 1932

Death in the Woods, 1933

No Swank, 1934

Puzzled America, 1935

Kit Brandon, 1936

Plays: *Winesburg and Others*, 1937

Home Town, 1940

The Intent of the Artist {with others}, 1941

Sherwood Anderson's Memoirs, 1942

Bibliography

Sherwood Anderson, *Sherwood Anderson's Notebook,* (New York, N.Y., Boni & Liveright, 1926)

Sherwood Anderson, *Sherwood Anderson's Memoirs,* (New York, N.Y., Harcourt, Brace and Company, 1942)

Howard Mumford Jones and Walter B. Rideout, *Letters of Sherwood Anderson,* (Boston, MA., Little, Brown and Company, 1953)

About the Author

Anna Maria Caldara has written extensively about the need for humanity to reconnect with the earth since the publication of her first book *Endangered Environments* in 1989. A long-time activist and journalist, her recent releases were *Gossamer Threads* (poetry), and *Lenape Culture in Stone and Wood*. She lives in Bangor, Pennsylvania, U.S.A.

Made in the USA
Middletown, DE
29 June 2016